# And She Sr

Scarlett Goodman

Copyright © 2016 by Scarlett Goodman

Cover design courtesy of Jean Hefner. Cover photo courtesy of Vladimir Nikulin, Masson Photography.

My first book, Peace for the Day, Quiet at Night, was dedicated to my wonderful parents. This book is dedicated to three men who have given me many reasons to smile.

My husband – you are the rock of love and security in my life. Thank you for your faithfulness to your family. Thank you for being such a wonderful husband and father, and for being the biggest supporter of my writing. I love you.

My brother - I loved you the moment I laid my nearly-five-year-old eyes on you for the first time. We have had a special, unbreakable bond all our life and no one makes me laugh like you do. I treasure our childhood memories and the trips we've been able to take as adults. I love you.

My son – you are an undeniable gift from God. You came wrapped in mystery and many years of prayer, and you are the joy of mine and your father's life. Every time I look at you, I'm reminded of God's perfect timing, and I know God has a wonderful design for your life. I love you more than words can say.

# FOREWORD

*And She Smiles at the Future*. What a refreshing thought! Scarlett titled this devotional book based on Proverbs 31:25, *"She is clothed with strength and dignity; she can laugh at the days to come"* (NIV). It's no irony that Scarlett relates to this particular scripture. My personal observation is that this scripture is an accurate description of Scarlett herself – a woman of great strength, integrity, and perseverance. A woman of sincere faith, who can smile at her future because she is focusing on the One who holds her days. Scarlett's faith is real. And because of that, the devotions that you are about to encounter will also be real.

Perhaps you struggle with the future. Maybe you have fear about the days ahead. You may be concerned about trusting God with the unknown. Staying in His Word, daily, will be vital for you. Just like it's unhealthy to skip a meal, or to go a day without water, skipping on the spiritual nourishment from God's Word will leave you spiritually dehydrated. If you've been dehydrated recently, you know the impact. Your brain is foggy, your thoughts are confused, your reflexes are poor, and you are vulnerable to discouragement. A spiritual dehydration is much the same. Do you *really* want to be able to smile at your future? Not a fake smile, but a genuine smile that requires no effort or manipulation? Do you want to have discernment and wisdom? Then keep yourself well nourished. This devotional guide is a great way to get started. Each day, Scarlett will present a scripture, and a short discussion that allows the scripture to become applicable to your daily tasks and struggles. Meet with God in the morning. Meet with Him in the evening. This pattern will facilitate a desire, and a routine, for meeting with Him throughout the day, as you encounter the various challenges that are sure to come.

Every day I encounter people who struggle with life's challenges. I often assign homework assignments. These are specific tasks that will assist them in accomplishing their goals, whether it is related to addiction, depression, anxiety, eating disorders, marital issues, etc... No matter the concern, being in God's Word is always a part of the answer. Often times, we need someone to take us by the hand and guide us to Him, to help us study His Word, or to gently introduce us to the Hope that is found in Him. This devotional book is an example of that type of tool. So, if you are struggling today, then I want to encourage you to consider this book part of your homework assignment. This is a great way to begin your journey with God, and to discover through Him, how one *really can* smile.

Scarlett, thanks for your obedience in using your incredible gift of writing to encourage God's people in their daily journey!

Donna Gibbs
Director, *A Clear Word Counseling Center*
Author of *Sacred Secrets to Healthy Relationships, Kiss and Tell, Faces of Hope, 30 Minutes to Stress Relief,* and co-author of *Water From the Rock.*

# INTRODUCTION

The title of this collection of devotionals is taken from Proverbs 31:25, *"Strength and honor are her clothing; and she shall rejoice in time to come."* Various commentaries often refer to the word *rejoicing* as either *smiling* or *laughing*. The powerful description in Proverbs 31 of a virtuous woman includes the fact that she has no fear of the future; in fact, she is so confident in Christ that she can actually smile at the days ahead, free of any anxiety or trepidation.

All our futures are uncertain to some degree: we don't know what a day may hold, what our health may be, or what joys or trials await us. We may have a practically perfect day when everything works in our favor, we sail through every traffic light, and we have time to spare, or we may experience a day of spilled coffee, flat tires, paper cuts, and other annoyances. More seriously, we may have a day of thrilling news or indescribable heartache; we just don't know what a day will bring.

Regardless of how we *feel*, we can still smile at the future because the future is controlled solely by God, and we trust Him because He is Lord of our lives. Since nothing is hidden from Him, He also sees all and providentially weaves His plan and purpose into everything we experience. Once we come to the place of totally accepting Him as supreme and sovereign, trust automatically follows suit and we get closer to a worry-free life. This doesn't mean that we'll never experience moments of fear or pain, but we can absolutely develop a life-pattern of dependence upon Him no matter what comes our way.

I wish I were more like the woman described in Proverbs chapter 31. Many women almost resent this woman who appears to embody everything we wish we could be, but one thing we often overlook is that this woman respected and obeyed the Lord. He took first place in her life. Because, and *only* because, she was firmly grounded in Christ, was she able to exemplify a strong and honorable life. We don't know if she was beautiful or popular or highly educated: instead we're told she is respected, industrious, and looks forward to the future with joy. She has a smile on her face, she laughs, and is not afraid of what she doesn't know for sure.

So then why are we afraid of the future? I think it's because we've allowed everything else to crowd out our commitment to the Lord. We attend church when it's convenient, we only read our Bible if we're desperate for an answer to prayer, we depend upon others to pray for us, and we try to fit in with everyone else by compromising what we know to be the truth.

Over the course of writing this book, I was faced with several circumstances that truly tested my ability to trust wholeheartedly. Despite those painful experiences, I can still say that Jesus is always faithful and that trust is a daily resolve to cast all our anxieties on Him. Many times I felt as if the best I could do was to put one foot in front of the other and trust Him for that step only. Even as I write this, I know many women facing similar trials of their faith and I pray that this book will be an encouragement. Please know that I understand the struggle of wondering why God doesn't always seem to answer our prayers right away or take away pain that we feel is almost too much to bear. I've learned to stay in the moment more and focus on the day instead of trying to predict the future and, in turn, worry about it. Life can be hard at times, but we serve a God able to carry our burdens when they're too much for us.

My prayer is that every woman who reads this book will be challenged to let go of any fears, anxieties, and worries about the future and instead cling to the promises we have in Christ. He is all we'll ever need and He wants us to smile, and even laugh, in confidence at the days ahead, no matter what they hold. Please join me as we smile together at the future, confident in our Savior's perfect plan. ☺

Scarlett Goodman

# HAPPY YELLOW DAYS

*"You are all children of light, and the children of the day: we are not of the night, nor of the darkness."*
I Thessalonians 5:5

I was talking with a friend the other day when I used an expression I'd never used before. I was describing a day in which everything seemed to work out flawlessly, when I referred to it as a, "happy yellow day". On that day in particular, I had felt good all day long and I'd not experienced any sort of delays or negativity. I'm not quite certain exactly how my mind came up with the phrase, but it perfectly captured the feeling. I've long associated the color yellow with happiness, light, and positivity. Maybe because I had a bright yellow bedroom as a little girl or maybe because I love yellow flowers, there is somehow an association for me that yellow equals happiness.

Ironically, a big trend in decorating and clothing over the past few years has been the combination of yellow and grey. The colors work beautifully together and I have seen at least one home decorated impeccably in these colors. It's ironic, in one sense, as yellow generally reminds people of happy things while grey brings up images of grey clouds and maybe even sadness. Together, however, the colors complement and balance each other in a tasteful way.

In today's verse, we see that believers in Christ are set apart as light, not darkness. While we may experience moments, and even seasons, of hardship or struggle, we are still safe in the care of our loving, heavenly Father. There is a happy condition or state of mind that all true Christians can rest in as we think about the future, firmly grounded by the anchor of God's protection. No matter who is elected President, what terrorist plots are carried out, or what disasters may occur all around the world, we serve the one true God who has all things providentially in His control. It's so easy nowadays to be fed news bits all day long (most of it tragic and upsetting) and begin to think that all is grey. Don't lose sight of the fact that we can be joyful and upbeat even in dire circumstances because we have the light of Christ within us.

I hope that the day or week ahead will be one full of happiness and unexpected, wonderful surprises for you. I truly hope some great news will come your way or you'll see a prayer answered! No matter what, don't forget that The Light of the World, Jesus Christ, is always working behind the scenes to give you an abundant life, no matter how you may *feel*. He is in control and His plan is always for the best. So, we don't just decorate with yellow and grey; we live it. If you do experience a happy yellow day sometime soon, please spread that same type of cheer, which cannot be diminished, as you interact with others.

But just in case you have a grey day sometime soon, don't forget the contrast of good that can be found in the darkest of circumstances and be reminded that the happiest days are ahead for us as Christians. One day we'll walk on streets paved in gold: Revelation 21:21b, *"...and the street of the city was pure gold, as it were transparent glass."* Can you really even begin to comprehend that? Let the future promises of God delight your thoughts today!

**What is God teaching me from today's devotional?**

# A BOX OF SURPRISES

*"Charm is deceitful and beauty is passing, but a woman who fears the Lord, she shall be praised."*
Proverbs 31:30

A fairly new trend for women today is to purchase boxes of certain beauty-related items that come in the mail on a regular basis. Officially referred to as 'subscription boxes', this relatively new idea includes everything from clothing to fragrances or the latest, greatest cosmetic products. Companies will package up just about anything to suit your individual taste, and even assign you a personal stylist as part of the bargain. I've personally subscribed to one of the clothing box companies for over a year and find it exciting to open up a box of surprises every four weeks! The idea is that you keep what you want and send back what you don't like. Some months I've been thrilled with the special delivery and others not so much, but I find that the surprise is the best part.

There's nothing wrong with wanting to put forward our best self, and that often involves some complimentary beauty products for our face, skin, and hair. It can also take some experimenting to find the best shades and formulations to suit our look and personal needs. That being said, any time we put our own self-importance (including our looks) above the things of Christ, we run the risk of creating an idol of our own making. It's a very subtle change from being reasonably concerned about our looks and health to being obsessed with our physical appearance. I heard one woman say that her first cosmetic surgery led to the next, which led to the next, only because she kept hoping for 'just a little better.' The enemy of good is better, right?

The Bible is very clear in today's passage that the true measure of a woman's beauty is her respect (or love) for the things of God. True beauty is always lit from within our souls. While it's important to look our best in a way that is Christ-honoring, our physical appearance is but one part of our whole person. It is our innermost reverence for the things of God that shows itself in the way we conduct our lives. In a society that places such strong importance on the things that help make us *look* pretty, isn't it refreshingly gratifying to remember what the Lord said in I Samuel 16:7, *"For the Lord does not see as man sees; for man looks at the outward appearance, but the Lord looks at the heart."* How much simpler our lives would be, and how much more fulfilling, if we focused on the heart!

    I pray that we will be challenged to reframe our perspective of what true beauty is from God's viewpoint. If Christ is looking at our hearts for beauty, what does He see? Is there kindness, compassion, gentleness, and selflessness or are we harboring sin that takes away from our beautiful spirit? Pray and ask the Lord for a right perspective of beauty and then seek to nurture the things that God desires for us to have inside. After all, shouldn't we be but reflections of the magnificent beauty that is Christ?

**What is God teaching me from today's devotional?**

# WHO DO YOU LOOK LIKE?

*"He who says he abides in Him ought himself also to walk just as He walked."*
1 John 2:6

Has anyone ever told you that you look like someone else? Be it a celebrity, a famous person from history, or even a person across town, it's always intriguing to hear that you bear a resemblance to someone else. Last year, I was wearing my hair up and had my glasses on when someone in a coffee shop told me I looked like Sarah Palin! I don't think I look like her at all, but that person thought I did. Within my own family, I've often heard that I look like my Aunt on my Father's side. When he was younger, many people used to say that my Dad looked like Elvis Presley! Physical similarities are interesting phenomena, aren't they?

Not long ago, while sitting at a stop light, I saw a woman in a Jeep next to me who looked exactly like Queen Elizabeth II. I'm serious, the resemblance was striking, and no, I hadn't had too much coffee that morning! Seeing "Queen Elizabeth" in a yellow Jeep next to me made me think a lot about the way in which we are sized up by our appearance. For better or worse, many a first impression is made primarily on how we look or present ourselves.

As Christians, we ought to all bear certain similarities to Christ with the way in which we live. After all, we are ambassadors for Him; quite literally, Christ-followers who strive to look like Him by our actions and attitudes. Where Jesus showed compassion, humility, and forgiveness, so should we. The peacefulness Jesus had in the midst of the storm is peace we can experience too as we learn to trust Him to carry us through. Every time we're tempted to give in to temptation, we should remember how Christ used scripture to defeat Satan, and then do the same thing ourselves.

While my hair, makeup, and clothes may project a certain image to the world, more than anyone else, I hope I look like Christ in the way I live my life. While I can never be perfect, I can (and should) strive to be as much like Him as possible. Today's verse in I John reminds us that, if we say we belong to Christ, then we should walk (live our life) as He did. Put another way, we should imitate Him in the way we show genuine love to others, the way we forgive, the things we stand for, and the things we avoid. We were created in His image, and if we've accepted Him as our Savior in faith, we should be more like Him over time as we deepen our relationship with Him.

No matter what color our hair or eyes, how much we weigh, or what time has done to our bodies, we have an eternal soul that is safely held in Christ's hands. I hope that the next time you look in the mirror you will see the amazing handiwork of God. I pray that you know your value in Him and that you won't choose anything that would cheapen or take away from His very best plan for your life. Then, set about making wise choices to live your life in a way that others will know you are a Christ-follower. Is there anything that could ever be more beautiful than that?

**What is God teaching me from today's devotional?**

# IN-BETWEEN TIMES & SEASONS

*"To everything there is a season, a time for every purpose under heaven:"*
Ecclesiastes 3:1

During the time in-between seasons of the year, it's not uncommon to feel a bit pulled in two directions. Temperatures, clothing styles, fresh foods, and nature all change to adjust to the next season. We may feel unsure from time to time which season we're in as we seem to have one foot in one season and one in the other. Especially when we have an unseasonably cold or warm day, we may really be confused.

I've been reminded recently about how often, in our personal lives, we are also caught somewhere between seasons. There are some very defined seasons like childhood, adolescence, college, first jobs, newly-married, career milestones, and retirement just to name a few. There are also seasons that break in and disrupt the way we think things should be, causing us to question why they would come at all: job loss, bankruptcy, death, broken relationships, and illness. Many people in their 40's describe themselves as belonging to the 'sandwich generation', sandwiched between the responsibilities of having children in school and parents who are aging. We are all doing our best to juggle the demands around us, but there are some days when our best efforts feel feeble. It's at these times that we're often torn between what we want to do, what's expected of us, and what we have to do to keep our finances and our relationships afloat. It can be an exhausting cycle of day-in-and-day-out without much respite.

Ecclesiastes chapter eleven is an oft-quoted Old Testament scripture reminding us that there are times or seasons of life that we all pass through. This *is* a time to be born. There *is* a time to die. There *is* a time for everything. God is never caught by surprise or unsure of what to do next.

He has a plan, a purpose, and a scheduled appointment that He will not break. We worry because we don't always understand *when* things will happen, when the seasons of our life will change, but if we trust Him, we can be assured that no matter when the seasons of life arrive, they will come at exactly the right time.

If you feel a little like you're in limbo, straddling the fence of one season or another of life, but not quite on either side, take comfort: you are not alone – many others are facing the same dilemma and Christ is always by your side. Take a moment right now to breathe deeply, lift your head to Heaven, close your eyes, and ask God to quiet your spirit so you can truly appreciate where you are in life. Instead of struggling against time, lean in to it and find all the joy you can in the season you're in now. Soon enough, it too will pass and you may find yourself wishing you'd enjoyed it a little more.

When my son was just a baby, my Mama said to me, *"All you have to worry about is today. Tomorrow will be there when the sun comes up again."* Her perspective was right on target. Christ didn't create us to be always begrudging or overly-anticipating the last or the next season of life. Jesus calls us into a relationship with Him that is relevant every moment of every day as we trust Him with both yesterday and tomorrow, the season past and the season yet to come.

**What is God teaching me from today's devotional?**

# HAIRSPRAY, FINGERNAILS, AND OTHER REASONS NOT TO GET IN A HURRY

*"Be still, and know that I am God; I will be exalted among the nations, I will be exalted in the earth!"*
Psalm 46:10

Just recently, my family had one of those mornings where we were in a rush to get out the door to church. It was the usual variety of feeling rushed: the kind where everywhere you look you see one more thing that needs to be done before you can leave home. Such was the case with my son and his fingernails. I had just finished spraying my hair (this point will be important shortly) when I noticed that my son's fingernails had apparently doubled in length overnight! His fingernails are a constant source of bewilderment and attention for me. First, I'm amazed at how quickly they grow, and secondly, I'm constantly trimming them!

As I was explaining, I'd walked out of the bathroom from spraying my hair, saw that his fingernails needed trimming, and immediately set to work to make sure he didn't leave the house with too-long nails. (I have nail trimming down to a science and so it was done in record time!) Just as we were about to leave the house, I took one quick glance in the mirror and noticed some strange specks of white in my hair. In what could only be called unbelievable, the front of my hair was speckled with tiny little fingernail clippings! I guess that as I was bent over his hands, the unusual combination of hairspray and rapid-fire trimming had resulted in some nail fragments going airborne into my sticky bangs! I stood in the bathroom and had a good laugh at myself as I picked the tiny fingernail clippings out of my hair.

Later on, I thought about how rushed I often feel as I try to get from Point A to Point B. It's easy to pile so much on ourselves that it's all we can do to move forward. While I wish I could slow things down, I don't always feel that it's within my power to do so. Is anyone relating here?

We are very clearly instructed in today's scripture to, *"Be still and know that I am God."* It is such a simple, profound Scripture, and yet it can feel very hard to do. I find that I often struggle with the *"be still"* part. I can be still for a few minutes, but being still long enough to really "know" God takes effort. God will not be rushed or fit into our schedule whenever and however we think He should. While He understands our struggle to hang on to the whirling schedules of our lives, He also calls us to seek Him first. If our tightly-wound agendas have such a strangle-hold on our time, we need to take a serious look at what is truly important. We most likely need to let some things go, not with the intent of replacing that time with something else, but rather to open up space in our lives for real communion with God.

One other thing occurred to me as I've pondered God's call for us to *"be still."* I find that I'm not always just rushing around because of commitments, but I'm often rushing to a conclusion when I need to step back and consider what God may be teaching me. I may feel bad and draw the conclusion that I'm at death's door. I may have a month of extraordinary expenses and come to the conclusion that the sky is falling. God never intends for us to get ahead of Him, but if we're rushing to a conclusion, we may try to decide an outcome before its time. Be still means to <u>be</u> <u>still</u>, which includes our mind's activity.

Try today to be very intentional about seeking to *"Be still and know."* Try reading Psalm 139 and then take time to ponder all the ways in which God intimately knows and understands you. Give all that rushing here and there to Him and watch expectantly for how He will help you slow down. Sometimes we just need to s-l-o-w d-o-w-n our pace, literally. Don't rush around your house or workplace, and don't speed in your vehicle. You can be intentional about what needs to be done without breakneck speed. Hurry often makes worry and worry isn't of God. I truly believe so many of our issues could be solved by just simply slowing down.

## What is God teaching me from today's devotional?

# TICK-TOCK UNWINDS THE CLOCK

*"My times are in Your hand; deliver me from the hand of my enemies, and from those who persecute me. Make Your face shine upon Your servant; save me for your mercies' sake."*
Psalm 31:15-16

▪▪▪▪▪▪▪▪▪▪▪▪▪▪▪▪▪▪▪▪▪▪▪▪▪▪▪▪▪▪▪▪▪▪▪▪▪▪

My mother once gave me some wonderful advice, in the way that only she could give. I was describing a situation in which I felt stressed and anxious, and she told me a story about something that helped her years ago when she was facing a similar situation. Mama said that she'd been feeling depressed as a young woman and had gone to the public library in search of a book that might help her. The book she chose, the title of which she's since forgotten, told the story of a woman who felt at her wits end. The woman in the book described sitting one day listening to the tick-tock of a clock and began to see herself as being wound so tightly that one more rotation of the proverbial clock inside her might cause her to burst into a jumble of pieces. The author proceeded to describe a thought which occurred to her at that moment and ended up changing her way of thinking. The thought went something like this, "Tick-tock unwinds the clock, tick-tock unwinds the clock…" For every tick of seconds passing, the clock was actually being *unwound*. My mother said that she began to think of the time given her as not actually ticking away *toward* a deadline or a cutoff, but rather as helping her unwind *away* from it.

Yes, we certainly all have demands and pressurized moments (some days more than others), but we don't have to allow them to consume us. Most everything, even the things that seem so critically important, can be accomplished in a way that isn't chaotic or driven by anxiety. I find that the things I fear most are almost always things somewhat manufactured by my over-zealous imagination. It's easy to allow one bad feeling, one day of defeat, one instance of unhappiness to chart the course of the next day and the day after that. Before long, the pattern of expectation is set and all your energy is spent trying to fend off the bad feelings that something worse might occur. It's a horrible, debilitating trap that many women fall prey to without even realizing it. The hard part is that once you're in that trap, it can feel nearly impossible to climb out.

    I cannot emphasize strongly enough the importance of telling yourself the truth during times when you feel that the sky is about to fall down on you. Speaking the truth of Who God Is becomes critical at moments when you're not sure if you're going to make it. Try saying out loud, "Do I believe God is good? Do I believe God can and will take care of me through this dark time in my life? Did God ever tell me to try to handle all my problems on my own? Does God desire to use my life to point others to Him? Do I trust God? Does God love me?" You could take this list and expand it however you'd like. At the end of the day, God is love. He desires to help you and not to harm you, to give you a future and a hope. He will intervene in ways you never imagined and He will help you.

    So, Mama's timeless (pun intended ☺) advice, along with her prayers and trust in God, helped me tremendously. If you're in a place where you feel there's no way out or that the darkness of anxiety or depression are robbing you of your life, please seek out a good, Christian counselor and work on the journey of getting out of the pit. And as you get better and better each day, remember that tick-tock unwinds the clock.

**What is God teaching me from today's devotional?**

# I KNOW HE CAN, BUT WILL HE?"

*"Ask, and it will be given to you; seek, and you will find; knock, and it will be opened to you. For everyone who asks receives, and he who seeks finds, and to him who knocks it will be opened. "Or what man is there among you who, if his son asks for bread will give him a stone? Or if he asks for a fish, will he give him a serpent? If you then, being evil, know how to give good gifts to your children, how much more will your Father who is in heaven give good things to those who ask Him!"*
Matthew 7:7-11

One of the greatest spiritual questions I've ever pondered has been this: *"I know He (God) can, but will He?"* I know God *can* resolve this issue I'm facing, I know He *can* calm the raging seas, I know He *can* work miracles, I know He *can* heal, but *will* He? Does my prayer request fit into His perfect design for my life, or am I praying in vain?

For the eight years we prayed for a child, my husband I carefully tiptoed around the subject of whether or not God would choose to answer our prayer. I think it was too painful to verbalize the fear that He wouldn't and yet equally as hurtful to think that perhaps it was for our good. During the last year or so of our wait, this question became more than a subconscious-level thought and turned into nearly an all-consuming quagmire. As those last days limped along, I began to wonder if it was time to put our prayers on the shelf, so to speak, and just give up. I questioned whether or not God even *wanted* me to stop praying. I wondered if I should stop begging for a child and refocus on something else. It was a painful, agonizing place to exist.

During the time of waiting for a child, like so many other dark days, God's guidance came shining through at exactly the right time. For me, comfort came late one night as I was reading Matthew 7:7-11, my tears soaking the pages of my Bible and my exhaustion reaching an all-time low. There in that lamp-lit room the words (and meaning) of this passage of Scripture seemed to leap off the page right into my heart. What I saw that night was that there was no mention of ceasing to pray, but rather a promise that an answer would come. I knew that night that no matter *what* the answer would be, it *would* indeed come. There would come a time when I would clearly know God's answer. That did happen, but it did take time. The lessons I learned during those hard times of waiting were so instrumental in my spiritual and emotional development that I truly cannot begin to express just how much God taught me over those years. They were wilderness years, for sure, but they proved priceless in the end.

I have no idea what you're facing right now. You, too, may be tempted to throw in the towel and call it quits on your prayers. You may feel that heaven is deaf to your cries and perhaps even that God has let you down. I can assure you that His presence is always with you and He knows where the journey you're on is leading. God cannot be bent to our time schedule and He won't be. He will always answer at exactly, precisely, and perfectly when the time is right. Until then, our only instruction, and the ultimate obedient act, is to trust Him.

**What is God teaching me from today's devotional?**

# IS IT EVER RIGHT TO DO WRONG TO DO RIGHT?

*"For the good that I will to do, I do not do; but the evil I will not to do, that I practice."*
Romans 7:19

*"Is it ever right to do wrong to do right?"* is a question I've heard credited to Dr. Bob Jones, Sr., and is intended to cause us to scrutinize our motives. For example, I heard of a child who once took money from an offering plate at church only to turn around and give it to a worthwhile charity. While seemingly innocuous in one sense, the child had still taken something that wasn't his to take. How about the person who justifies telling a lie to smooth over a situation, or how about the person who takes shortcuts at work to get ahead, all with the good intent of providing for their family? Is that any different? What about the parent who shows favoritism to one child over another, all because the favored child is more like them in personality? You see, very often things appear one way and are actually something else entirely.

In a similar vein, we've all found ourselves in situations where the very thing we intended to do, we didn't do, while the thing we most wanted to avoid doing, was the very thing we did. It sounds a bit like talking in circles, but it actually makes perfect sense. The Apostle Paul wrote the book of Romans to the thriving church in ancient Rome, and in today's passage of Scripture, Paul openly shares the struggle of his desire to do good and then, at times, his seeming inability to do so. Christians throughout the ages have nodded in agreement as they've read his words because we can identify with his dilemma. It can be easy to justify one wrong if we see the greater good being accomplished, yet God still asks us to examine our hearts against His Word. Does the Bible ever condone sin? Are there exceptions? God, in His all-knowing, loving nature has provided guidelines for us to protect us. His guidance for our lives will never include compromise or bargaining with Him for our way over His.

So, instead of looking for loopholes or other ways to try and bend the Bible to what we'd like it to say, let's all recommit to obedience. Following God's direction for our lives will far outweigh any temporary (and unfulfilling) compromise of the truth. Remember Jesus' words in John 8:32, *"And you shall know the truth, and the truth shall make you free."* Truth is always its own defense. When you tell yourself the truth about any situation, you immediately invite right responses.

Sometimes it takes a lot of courage to look squarely at the truth and accept it. Perhaps debt has you positively strangled and yet you continue to spend as if there should be no constraints on your budget. Maybe your health is in jeopardy but you refuse to take the steps necessary to improve it. Perhaps you've compounded one problem with another and have justified them both because you're hurting. Maybe you've filled your life with activity on top of activity in an attempt to drown out a piece of your life that seems just too hard to face. We all encounter problems of all sorts at various seasons of life, but please remember this: Christ is the answer. You can face the truth, believe the truth, and overcome whatever you're facing with the Lord's help. Give your questions to Him for He has all the answers.

**What is God teaching me from today's devotional?**

# SOCKS THAT DON'T MATCH AND OTHER NONESSENTIALS

*"For this is the love of God, that we keep His commandments. And His commandments are not burdensome."*
1 John 5:3

I tried so hard one day not long ago to get my son to wear socks that matched his outfit. We were on our way to a special event, and I thought he should look a certain way. Despite my best efforts, he begged and pleaded with me to the contrary. He wanted to wear his Captain America socks and was trying everything in his power to convince me that the other socks just wouldn't work. At one point, he even told me that, if he could wear the socks he wanted to wear, he would eat all his vegetables for a month! It had been a long day already, and I finally conceded, deciding that it wasn't worth the argument I was having over mere knitted footwear. Sure, I could have insisted, laid down the law, and refused to take no for an answer, but right then I just needed to let it go. The event was the important thing, not that he was perfectly matched. So, I took him up on the vegetable promise, and he walked out the door with a pale green shirt, black shorts, and red, white, and blue socks. When we arrived at our destination, several kids were in equal states of mismatch, and I laughed to myself at just how silly the Great Sock Debate had been.

As petty as this story may seem, we all find ourselves majoring on the minor from time to time. We argue, debate, and dig in our heels over all sorts of things that don't really merit such intense, dogmatic fortitude. For some, if every dinner isn't organic, balanced, and farm-to-table, we feel we've let our family down. For others, if every holiday spent with our family isn't perfect, we feel as if something is wrong and it's up to us to fix it. More seriously, we can believe that we have to mend every hurt that our children or spouse encounter, or that we have to try and "appear" to have it all together, even when we're dying on the inside. At the end of the day, it's worth asking the person we see in the mirror whether or not what matters so much *really* matters *so much*.

God tells us in the Bible that there are some things which hold eternal significance. He also instructs us to let go of things that are only our *version* of important. It's interesting how we pass through seasons of thinking things are important, even essential, and then our focus passes on to something else. For instance, I used to always kept my nails perfectly done, and then I discovered that I preferred to work in the yard more than I cared about my nails being just-so. My priorities changed over time and what had seemed so important at one time eventually lost its hold on me. I still appreciate and admire well-manicured nails on others, but it's just not a priority with me anymore.

Keeping God's commandments is what matters. Trusting Him with the very core of your soul is what matters. Matching socks and perfect nails, while not bad things at all, aren't what <u>really</u> matter. I challenge all of us to memorize today's verse of scripture. Are we living our life in obedience to God and in keeping with what He has instructed us to do? If not, let's confess that and strive to move forward in submission to Him. A life spent in the pursuit of things that have eternal significance will give you joy in a way that nothing temporary will ever be able to give.

**What is God teaching me from today's devotional?**

# THE FALLEN BIRD

*"Are not two sparrows sold for a copper coin? And not one of them falls to the ground apart from your Father's will. But the very hairs of your head are all numbered. Do not fear therefore; you are of more value than many sparrows."*
Matthew 10:29

*"Look at the birds of the air, for they neither sow nor reap nor gather into barns; yet your heavenly Father feeds them. Are you not of more value than they? Which of you by worrying can add one cubit to his stature?*
Matthew 6:26-27

I truly believe that God sometimes chooses to speak to us in mysterious ways. A while back, I was standing in my kitchen, praying about a heavy burden on my heart. I had actually just asked God to show me that everything was going to be ok, when I heard a very loud *thump!* against the kitchen window. The sound so startled me that I jumped and turned quickly to see what had caused such a loud noise. At first I saw nothing, but seconds later noticed a helpless, little bird lying on the ground, clearly having a hard time breathing and in distress. In an instant, God placed on my mind today's Scripture passages found in the gospel of Matthew. As I stared at that small, brown bird, nearly camouflaged in the mulch outside my kitchen window, my eyes filled with tears as I thought of Christ's words.

God reminded me that morning, in a very real sense, that He knows about the birds and about me. (There's a happy ending to this story in that the bird did appear to recover and was eventually able to fly away!) The experience of my prayer and the bird falling to the ground reminded me, again, that God knows all. He is our wonderful, trustworthy God. The Wycliffe Bible Commentary, with respect to Matthew 10:29 states, "...*without*

*His providential direction not even such insignificant events can occur."* If God orders the smallest of events in life, is this not a further antidote to fear?

Fear is a force that we reckon with every single day. It's interesting that Jesus tells us not to fear and then reminds us of our value to Him. Very often fear and worry are used in close proximity. One seems to fuel the other and before long we can be swept up in a cycle of both. Remember that fear and worry are not of God; they are tools Satan uses to hurt, cripple, and defeat us. Jesus says that perfect love casts out fear. Love can't abide fear and fear can't stand in the face of true love.

It can be very disheartening for Christians that we live in a time when God's ways are ridiculed and ignored. It can also be a time of anxiety over the future. I hope today's Scripture will remind you that there is a providential design behind the scenes of our human understanding and that God is always vigilant in His precise control over the affairs of mankind. We can trust Him! I don't know what you may be facing today, but I do know, and completely believe, that nothing ever surprises God. We do wrong to ever look at Christ with an eye of suspicion or doubt. Don't ever quit waging war against the negative thoughts that creep in and seek to have us question God. I hope we will all seek to live our life in a way that is pleasing to Him, and that we will rest confidently in the assurance that, though we may see difficulty and pain all around us, God is faithful and He can be trusted.

**What is God teaching me from today's devotional?**

# A CHRISTMAS TREE IN JULY

*"But Mary kept all these things and pondered them in her heart."*
Luke 2:19

This past year, we were able to get a fantastic deal on a "Christmas in July" sale, and so our new Christmas tree arrived the last week of July. It was one of those pre-lit, instant-power trees with no cord to fool with or wires to disentangle. I wanted to be sure it would work so up went the tree in our Living Room. Despite being a replication of the real thing, it really was beautiful with all its multi-colored lights, fresh new limbs, and perfect artificial pinecone placement throughout. It was so nice, in fact, that we kept it up for nearly a week. I'm sure the neighbors, if they caught a passing glance through the front window, either thought the house was on fire or we'd lost our minds and put up a Christmas tree in the middle of July!

Several times over those few days, I found myself looking at the tree and wishing that it was Christmas-time. While the summer season is wonderful for many reasons, there's just no season quite like Christmas. I found myself longing for the inspiration of the holiday season in which we celebrate Christ as a baby, wrapped in swaddling clothes, and laying in a manger. With the anticipation of school starting back and the long, warm days, December felt like a long way off in the distance.

The truth, of course, is that the Christmas season is one we celebrate in our hearts. It's an attitude of peace and goodwill that transcends time and causes us to feel a true connection to our fellow man. In Luke 2:19, we're told that Mary was so overwhelmed by the events of baby Jesus' birth, that she tucked those special memories away in her heart and thought of them often. What if we were to carry the awe and wonder of that special time of year with us in the middle of July (and the whole year through, for that matter)? What if we thought often of the real significance of Christ becoming man, bound for the cross, so that we might be reconciled to Him?

Christmas <u>will</u> be here before we know it, but I pray that we won't keep the spirit of Christmas in a box, so to speak, to be pulled out only once a year. I hope that we will each, often and sincerely, think of the beauty and wonder of that most-celebrated season and ask the Lord how we might direct others to Him. Just like the sweet little Christmas pageants that children participate in, dressed as angels, shepherds, wise men, and the holy family, we are also representatives of those who welcomed Christ at the very first Christmas. I pray that our light will shine brightly as we lead the way for others from darkness into His glorious light. As you go about your day and before you go to bed tonight, ponder, like Mary, the true Light of the World and treasure the anticipation of Christmas.

**What is God teaching me from today's devotional?**

# AN EMPTY FIELD

*"Now hope does not disappoint, because the love of God has been poured out in our hearts by the Holy Spirit who was given to us."*
Romans 5:5

My husband and I prayed for a very long time for a child. We suffered through eight years of infertility treatments, multiple medical procedures and surgeries, and the awful agony of waiting. During that time, my prayers took shape in different ways: sometimes pleading, sometimes frustrated, and sometimes lying face down on the floor in a pool of tears. I tried my best to avoid baby showers, Mother's Day and Father's Day activities, and anything else that reminded me of the fact that I wasn't a Mother. During one of those years, my husband's father died unexpectedly just a few short months after my only pregnancy ended in miscarriage, and it seemed as if the sky was falling in on us.

During those years, on my regular route to and from work, I would pass a certain, very large, corn field nearly every day. One day in particular, while passing by the corn field, I prayed and asked God to give me a sign concerning a child. This may sound silly to some of you, but I felt desperate to have some certainty that our struggles were going to be relieved. I prayed specifically that I would see a man walking though the field. I told God that if I saw that happen, then I would know we were going to one day have a child. I also prayed that if I saw two men walking through the field, then I would know that it wasn't going to happen and so I would just accept it.

Days turned to months, which turned to years. The corn grew, the corn was harvested, and the field was barren. The corn grew, the corn was harvested, and the field was barren. Once or twice I saw tractors, but not one time did I ever see anyone walking through the corn field. Even on the day we brought our son home, my husband drove past that corn field, and all we saw were corn stalks waving in the wind. I believe with all my heart that God heard every prayer I made, and I believe that He could have spoken however He chose if that was the best thing for my good and His glory. God, in His awesome sovereignty, simply and always, knows better than we do.

Now, many years later, I still occasionally pass that corn field. A sense of nostalgia sweeps over me for a moment every time I pass it as I recall the years of anticipation. The truth is that our hope in God doesn't rest in signs or what our eyes can physically see. No, God asks us to have faith in HIM alone. He asks us to leave the empty fields of our lives in His hands. I wish now I had not focused so much on what I thought I needed, but instead had trusted Him completely. Whatever you're praying for that seems to have gone a long time unanswered is not unheard. Please believe that! All the while I was looking and waiting for a sign in that field, God was at work behind the scenes designing a miracle. He is doing the same for you. Believe that and trust Him. The surprise gift of our son was so miraculous that no sign in any field could have ever compared.

**What is God teaching me from today's devotional?**

# UNCHARTERED TERRITORY

*"And I will bring the blind by a way that they knew not; I will lead them in paths that they have not known: I will make darkness light before them, and crooked things straight. These things will I do unto them, and not forsake them."*
Isaiah 42:16

■■■■■■■■■■■■■■■■■■■■■■■■■■■■■■■■■■■■

Indulge me a moment in a brief history refresher: On July 4, 1803, the territory of the United States literally doubled in size. When negotiations between Napoleon Bonaparte and third President of the United States, Thomas Jefferson, were all said and done, the US acquired the Louisiana Purchase for $15 million – that's 3 cents per acre of land (can you even imagine?). Covering land west of the Mississippi River from New Orleans through Montana, the new territory was almost entirely unknown to Americans at that time. Jefferson persuaded Congress to allocate $2,500 to his secretary, Meriwether Lewis, his friend, William Clark, and 31 others, known as the "Corps of Discovery", to explore the new territory.

The expedition finally set sail on May 14, 1804. Heading up the Missouri River, the Corps of Discovery began their now-famous explorations, which would continue over the next two years. The Corps recorded over 400 new plants and animals previously unknown in the East. Among these were many of the species for which the West is now known, such as antelope, prairie dogs, and grizzly bears. You may recall that the Shoshone Indian, Sacagawea, was the only female on the expedition and she served as the interpreter for many of the group's trading with other Indians.

Notes from the Lewis and Clark Expedition, as it later came to be known, revealed that each mile traveled was an adventure deep into unchartered territory where danger or opportunity might have been right around the next corner. It was wild country and there was no telling what the group may encounter. Several things I've read recorded sickness, fear, danger, and yet unparalleled excitement over the new discoveries being made daily. It's a fascinating story.

We, too, sometimes enter into unchartered territory in our own lives. With or without warning, we may find ourselves thrust into a new experience, completely foreign to us. Unwittingly, we become explorers of the new life put before us and we're often unsure of where to turn or what to expect. If you've ever suffered through a sudden onset of illness, the loss of a job, the reversal of fortune, or the unexpected loss of a loved one by death, divorce, or estrangement, you know what I'm referring to here. There are other examples also, but anything that is new to us can feel overwhelming, frightening, and unsettling.

Our scripture today reminds us that God is our ultimate Guide at times in which the way ahead is unknown, dark, and full of winding pathways. We'd so much prefer a straight line in which we could see the end ahead, but God has never given us the ability to see the future. That's another reason why worrying about it is so useless. Worry can never ever, ever, ever, ever change the future. God tells us that He controls the future and He wants us to depend upon Him daily, one step at a time, for the path ahead. When we keep our mind, our focus, and our energy on doing His will today, tomorrow will diminish in its ability to flame our imaginations.

**What is God teaching me from today's devotional?**

# UNATTACHED

*"For we brought nothing into this world, and it is certain we can carry nothing out."*
I Timothy 6:7

Last winter, two seemingly unrelated events came together in my life at something of a bizarre intersection. Though unconnected at first glance, both left me with the reminder of a deep spiritual truth. It all began when I did a much needed closet cleanout resulting in two very large bags of clothes designated as giveaways. As I picked through the sweaters, blouses, and jackets that had once been new and beautiful, I was struck by how worn-out clothes can look over a relatively short amount of time. There were a few things that I had worn a lot, but most of them were things that ended up not fitting quite right or just not appealing to me. So goes the fate of clothes…

It was the next event, however, that really took me by surprise! During that week's polar vortex of winter weather that sent temperatures into the negative numbers and crippled many parts of the country, the biting wind was indeed brutal. I was driving to work one of those mornings on my normal route, praying all the way for safety. It's easy to fall into auto pilot mode when you travel a familiar course on a regular basis, but that morning I was in a state of heightened awareness for fear of black ice. It was way before sunrise and there were very few cars out. The wind was whipping all around me and I could see the silhouette of trees bending unnaturally. Just as I rounded a familiar turn of the road, something caught my eye in the straightaway some distance ahead. From that distance it looked like many little clumps of colored objects blowing all over the road. Instinctively I slowed down and proceeded cautiously. What I realized a minute later was that I was in the stretch of road right across from a very large cemetary and the wind had blown all the artificial flowers into the road. They were everywhere – all over the road, in the ditch, probably even some in trees! It was an unusual sight to say the least.

The rest of the way to work that morning I was struck by many thoughts about what I'd just witnessed. I thought about the person whose job it would be to gather all those flowers in sub-zero weather, and I realized that there was no way the proper flowers would all be returned to their original spot. I thought about those bags of old clothes that were in my car with me that morning. One word, "unattached", kept coming to my mind. Those flowers, like everything else, will one day be unattached to us when we die. As our Scripture today reminds us, we will not take one thing with us from here. Things are just things. Placing exaggerated value on "stuff" always ends up in futility because enough stuff is never enough stuff. The things we do in Jesus' name, the obedient Christian life, those we point toward Christ – those are treasures that we do store in Heaven. *Matthew 6:19-21, "Do not lay up for yourselves treasures on earth, where moth and rust destroy and where thieves break in and steal; but lay up for yourselves treasures in heaven, whether neither moth nor rust destroys and where thieves do not break in and steal. For where your treasure is, there you heart will be also."*

Once we've prayed in faith and come to Christ as His child, we know that this life is not to be lived for ourselves only. We can live a life unattached to our things because our hope is not in temporal things, but in the eternal. And speaking of attachment, remember this – as a Christian, God will always be with you. *Romans 8:38-39, "For I am persuaded, that neither death, nor life, nor angels, nor principalities, nor powers, nor things present, nor things to come, nor height, nor depth, nor any other creature, shall be able to separate us from the love of God, which is in Christ Jesus our Lord."* Take comfort in knowing that this life is but a speck on the map of eternity. Make your life count for Christ!

**What is God teaching me from today's devotional?**

# STUMBLES AND RECOVERY

*"You ran well. Who hindered you from obeying the truth?"*
Galatians 5:7

At times, it can seem as if life isn't very forgiving of our mistakes, and yet we're all human therefore mistakes are bound to be made. Granted, some mistakes may be costlier than others, but we sometimes go about life under the cloud of attempted perfection. It is assumed that we should be able to do all things well and so we heap stress and anxiety upon ourselves as we buy into the deception that we've got to be excellent at everything. Sometimes that stress alone causes mistakes to happen! The point is that we all stumble and fail from time to time.

As hard as we may try, we'll never have a completely dust-free home, and we'll never achieve perfection at work. Our families will be flawed, and there will always be days that try our best efforts and leave us in tears. We shouldn't view life as a competition to appear to have it 100% together either. Only God is perfect and He knows that we are not. What He does ask is that we trust Him with the plan for our life and the direction He wants to give us, with all the seemingly imperfect turns it will inevitably take. This is not, however, an excuse to stray because God will provide the grace and faith we need to live an abundant Christian life if we'll just yield to His authority.

When the Apostle Paul wrote his letter to the Galatian church, he was very concerned that they not embrace falsehood. He wanted them to break free of legalism and grab hold of the spiritual freedom in Christ. In today's verse, Paul asks the early church a question that has been asked of Christians from generation to generation, *"Who hindered you?"* Put another way, *"What caused you to stumble?"* These people had indeed started well, but then became sidetracked by their detour outside of God's will. Paul was attempting to provide a course correction so that they might regain the ground they'd lost when they stumbled.

There are occasions when we may even become complacent about our faith. Sometimes we are tired and allow the circumstances of life to hinder our spiritual growth. Sometimes we allow sin to creep into our lives in very subtle ways: little white lies turn into major deceptions, the smallest bit of gossip becomes a full-scale drama, and missing church from time to time turns into only attending church from time to time. The smallest compromise, unchecked and unrepented, can quickly turn into a serious problem. The truth is that many situations stand ready to lure us away from a close walk with Christ: decisions made without prayer, greed, revenge, peer pressure, materialism, pride, etc. We have to guard our hearts with all diligence.

Despite our stumbles and falling short, we are reminded in Philippians 3:13b, that we can have a fresh start in Christ, *"…forgetting those things which are behind and reaching forward to those things which are ahead."* As you read this today, I hope your prayer will be that God will show you any area of your life which you need to recommit to Him. Yes, we <u>will</u> miss the mark and fall short of perfection, and that is exactly why we all need … a Savior.

**What is God teaching me from today's devotional?**

# FINDING THE GOOD

*"Therefore, thus says the Lord: If you return, then I will bring you back; you shall stand before Me; If you take out the precious from the vile, you shall be as My mouth. Let them return to you, but you must not return to them."*
Jeremiah 15:19

Many women have asked me for prayer from time to time and have shared how they've struggled with, or been affected by, some type of betrayal. These women have been grandmothers and new moms alike, crossing many boundaries of age and experience. Whether it be extramarital affairs, rebellious children, a difficult co-worker, or the disloyalty of anyone they had felt they could trust, one thing is clear – many people have suffered, either directly or indirectly, as a result of betrayal. Time after time, I've heard women say that they never thought it would happen to them. My heart breaks with those who've been subjected to the agony of this type of emotional upheaval in their lives.

The Lord showed me today's beautiful verse in Old Testament scripture as a rock of refuge in dealing with unfaithfulness. Let's look at the central part of the verse together, taken from the New American Standard translation – *"And if you extract the precious from the worthless, you will become my spokesman."* In a review of this verse in the Wycliffe Bible Commentary, I read that Jeremiah was being challenged to discipline his thoughts and speech so that he could then be God's spokesman to those around him. The end of the verse is actually a command not to sink to the level of those to whom he would be trying to help. Not that Jeremiah was better than anyone or without sin himself, but Jeremiah had to be on guard not to fall *into* sin when trying to help someone else *out* of it.

There is always good that can be gleaned and developed through difficulties of any sort. We gain confidence because of uncertainty, courage out of fear, trust out of darkness, and beauty out of betrayal. I'm sure you can think of a situation all your own in which you've witnessed first-hand the joy when good comes from bad. I love that Jeremiah is told by God that IF he could pull the good from the bad, he could THEN become a spokesperson for God. I believe that anytime we seek the positive from the negative we can share that experience in such a way as to significantly impact others. We are all, as Christians, called to be ambassadors (or spokespersons) for God. The particular experiences of our lives give us our own unique platform.

Isn't it like a drink of cold water on a hot day to talk with someone who knows the pain you've experienced or are experiencing? No matter what the trying issue, we take the good we've gained and we encourage others. The encouragement we receive can be passed on again and again, as our influence is felt. Your voice matters. When we seek God and the opportunities He will provide, we can truly be His spokesperson for good. Let us not too quickly forget Romans 8:28, *"And we know that all things work together for good to those who love God, to those who are the called according to His purpose."* My prayer for all of us is that we will find the good out of the darkest of places and then use that experience to help others. You are not alone!

**What is God teaching me from today's devotional?**

# NOWHERE TO RUN, NOWHERE TO HIDE

*"Keep me as the apple of Your eye; hide me under the shadow of Your wings,"*
Psalm 17:8

▪▪▪▪▪▪▪▪▪▪▪▪▪▪▪▪▪▪▪▪▪▪▪▪▪▪▪▪▪▪▪▪▪▪▪▪▪▪▪▪▪▪▪▪▪▪▪

When my son was just transitioning from toddler to little boy, he went through a phase of watching classic, western television shows like *Gunsmoke* and *Bonanza,* and he loved to dress like a cowboy around the house. One of the many things he learned from watching those old shows was the phrase, *"You've got nowhere to run and nowhere to hide."* One of his favorite things was to play hide and go seek, and then quote his newly-learned phrase whenever he found me. I could tell by his little grin that he took great pleasure in letting me know that I was cornered!

Hiding is one of the three avenues we may follow when in a calamitous situation. We can either run, hide, or fight. For most of us, running is the natural instinct, but hiding can be as well. Fighting is the hardest and the one thing we all hope we'll never have to do. I must admit that every time I'm in a stadium, a concert hall, a theatre, or any other place for that matter, I'm conscientious of the exits and the hiding places. Even in my own home, we've often talked through escape plans in the event of a fire. It's something I learned a long time ago during a self-defense class in college and something I've never forgotten. Nowadays it's often referred to as being in a state of "heightened awareness" – being keenly aware of your circumstances at all times.

Figuratively speaking, we all need a place to hide from time to time. We may not be running or hiding to protect our life, but we often are tired and weak from the struggles of our day to day and week to week experiences. David prayed in today's Scripture that he might be hidden under the protection of almighty God. David spent many years being chased by King Saul, and he recognized that no cave, no cloak of disguise, or any other attempt to conceal himself could give him the security that being in God's care could provide.

Colossians 3:3b tells us, *"...and your life is hidden with Christ in God."* In other words, once we become a Christian, our lives are deposited with Christ in a whole new spiritual realm. We should therefore seek after things that are part of God's plan and not our own selfish pursuits. I love to do word studies in scripture, and recently I've been personally challenged to learn all I can about what the Bible has to say about hiding and being hidden. There's so much to learn!

The next time your energy is spent and your 24-hour day just doesn't seem like it's enough, run to God and hide yourself under the shadow of his wings for protection and comfort. He is waiting to give you the quiet moments of rest that only come by communion with Him. It's not a formula or a mystic experience, but just close your eyes and run into His arms through prayer for all the love you will ever need. You will find that you DO have somewhere to run and somewhere to hide; in fact, it's the safest, most secure place of all.

**What is God teaching me from today's devotional?**

# ABIGAIL: A LESSON FOR ALL OF US

*"Charm is deceitful and beauty is passing, but a woman who fears the Lord, she shall be praised. Give her of the fruit of her hands, and let her own works praise her in the gates."*
Proverbs 31:30-31

• • • • • • • • • • • • • • • • • • • • • • • • • • • • • • • • • • • • • • • • • • • • • • •

The Old Testament passage of I Samuel chapter 25 tells the intriguing story of Abigail, the intelligent beauty who was the wife of Nabal, a wealthy, yet overbearing, man whose foolishness cost him his life. Because most marriages of her day were arranged years in advance, Abigail probably entered into that union through no choice of her own. We can only guess that Nabal's harshness and rudeness had made her life miserable. The name Nabal actually means "foolish", and the Hebrew word used here for *fool* actually denotes more than mere senselessness, but also moral perversity. When Nabal insulted David, the future king of Israel, and his men, Abigail's keen discernment and swift intervention persuaded David and won him over. Not long after this encounter, Nabal was dead at the hand of the Lord and David took Abigail as his wife. It's an interesting story that is fascinating to study!

Abigail may have appeared to have it all: beauty, wealth, intelligence, and status, yet her life at home was far from ideal. She had no doubt learned to make excuses for her husband and was an expert at pacifying bad situations. We can only imagine that she had a public face that hid the turmoil going on in her home. The brief narrative we're given of Abigail teaches us many lessons. She had learned how to make the best out of a difficult situation and she used her God-given wisdom to navigate through the toughest of times. By keeping a cool head and extending hospitality, she stands as a ready reminder to us today that we too can put our faith into action in the hard times.

So how does this Old Testament story apply to women today? First of all, I believe Abigail's life shows that none of us have it all together. Despite the book's cover, the inside of the story revealed a woman with a secret life at home; hers was a life of struggle and endurance, that many on the outside were probably unaware existed. After all, she was married to a wealthy man so I'm sure she probably had things that others couldn't afford. Also, Abigail's story shows us that humility, hospitality, and reverential deference can go a long way in honest negotiating. Abigail could have easily become a bitter, resentful woman and most of us wouldn't have blamed her. Instead, she had real faith and lived her life in the wisdom and fear of God. Another powerful lesson of her story is each of us is responsible for our own actions. Her husband answered for his actions and she was responsible for her own.

Whatever difficult situation you may think is hidden from everyone else and is your own secret problem, be reminded of Abigail; God didn't forget her and He won't forget you. There is a special hope for the woman of faith who depends upon the wisdom and power of God, and this hope does not disappoint. Christ knows the deepest needs of our heart and meets them in the way only He can. Intelligence, wealth, beauty, and status are all things we admire, but the woman that trusts in the Lord – she will be praised!

**What is God teaching me from today's devotional?**

# A LESSON IN TRUST

*"Then she made a vow and said, 'O Lord of hosts, if You will indeed look on the affliction of Your maidservant and remember me, and not forget Your maidservant, but will give Your maidservant a male child, then I will give him to the Lord all the days of his life..."*
I Samuel 1:11a

∎∎∎∎∎∎∎∎∎∎∎∎∎∎∎∎∎∎∎∎∎∎∎∎∎∎∎∎∎∎∎∎∎∎∎∎∎∎∎∎∎∎∎∎∎∎∎

The story of Hannah is one much-loved by Christian women the world over because it speaks of sorrow, triumph, and God's answers to our prayers. Hannah was unable to bear children yet tenderly loved by her husband, Elkanah, despite her infertility. However, we often overlook the price of her vow to the Lord. Even though Hannah was ultimately blessed with a child, Samuel, she essentially gave him in complete faith back to God for the Lord's service. As our verse today shows us, Samuel would be consecrated as a Nazarite for his entire life in service to God. In fact, Samuel was only about two or three years old when Hannah took him to Eli, the High Priest at that time, to serve in the temple.

The other day as I was reading this passage of scripture I was struck by one aspect of this beautiful story that had escaped me before. Eli had two very evil sons who served along with him in the temple. In fact, their reputation for wrongdoing was so well known throughout Israel that certainly Hannah and Elkanah would have known about it (I Sam. 2:22-25). Even though Eli's son's sins eventually cost them their lives, I wonder if Hannah worried about the home that her little son was going to, and I wonder if she considered what he might have been exposed to that was now beyond her control. We know that she took him a little coat every year (I Sam. 2:19), but beyond that she probably didn't see him. She had given Samuel, utterly and completely, in total faith to God.

If your child or grandchild, or a child you love, is in a situation today that is less than ideal, take comfort in Hannah's faith. Even more, take comfort in Hannah's God; the same God we serve today is able to care for our children even when they're away from us and even if they're in difficult circumstances. Hannah truly saw Samuel as a gift from God and she undoubtedly saw herself as the guardian of that gift for a time. As hard as it is for us to sometimes accept, our children belong to God and He entrusts us as their guardian for a time. If we have children, we should be training them to serve God and to be independent adults. Samuel grew to be one of the greatest Hebrew prophets and, as the last judge of Israel, he was revered as one of the greatest leaders Israel ever knew. Remember, Samuel was an instrumental and highly-influential figure in King David's life. His life had purpose and meaning from his conception until his death.

Just as Hannah gave Samuel to the Lord as a child, take a moment to pray today for your children or children you love and ask God's blessings on them. Every time we are separated from our children, whether just for a short time, the workday, or for longer periods of time, God is at work for their good and His glory. You are not parenting your child alone: God is always there, both wherever you are and wherever they are.

**What is God teaching me from today's devotional?**

# NOT ONLY FOR A DAY

*"Do not boast about tomorrow, for you do not know what a day may bring forth."*
Proverbs 27:1

Lots of things are only for a day. My husband recently celebrated a milestone birthday and, though there was cake and presents and family around to visit, it still only lasted one day. Parents and students spend a lot of time planning and preparing for prom and graduation, and yet those events will only be for a day. If the occasion is a happy one, we may wish the day could go on forever. If the day was difficult, it may have seemed as if it would never end. Without a doubt, special days should be celebrated in thanksgiving for all God has done for us. It's important to make a big deal out of birthdays, anniversaries, milestones of many sorts, and other important days. The difficult days we experience, while often just endured, are reminders that we can trust God in any circumstance.

The truth is that most of our days are of the ordinary variety, spent doing all the necessary things required of us to support our families, maintain our homes, and just keep the wheel of our life turning as it should. It's not uncommon for people to have weeks that are pretty much the same as the week before with little to differentiate it from all the others.

I was recently inspired by Psalm 42:8, *"The Lord will command His lovingkindness in the daytime, and in the night His song shall be with me – a prayer to the God of my life."* In this beautiful verse we are reminded that God is not just the God of our days and nights, but He's also the God of our entire life. All too often we tend to put our relationship with the Lord on the backburner when things are going well. When we're healthy, when our bank account looks good, when our family is at peace – these are the times that some people begin to mistakenly look in the mirror and unconsciously praise themselves. We can get sucked into a belief that our business acumen, our good timing, and our careful planning is the cause for our success. Without meaning to, we forget to praise God for His blessings and provision. When things aren't so rosy, when we're in pain, when we've experienced a tragedy – then our faith is really put to the test and we have to purposely decide to praise God in the storm.

Perhaps you're anticipating a day that will bring you happiness: a marriage, a child, a new job, a major purchase, a vacation, retirement, and the list could go on and on. No matter what you're looking forward to experiencing, remember that God is with you through it all. He is the God of your entire life. He is with you every single moment of every single day. No act of yours or mine escapes His notice and no prayer goes unheard. When we're standing in line, waiting in traffic, talking to our family, watching television, working, eating, sleeping – He Is There. Think of that for a moment...

I truly believe that if we could grasp with our hearts the significance of the fact that Christ is walking with us everywhere and at all times, it would change us. Stop what you're doing right now and take a moment to soak in the words of Psalm 46:10a, *"Be still, and know that I am God..."* Now, take that same quietness of spirit and approach this day with a renewed sense of Who designed it especially for your good and His glory.

**What is God teaching me from today's devotional?**

# THREE DAYS WITHOUT HIM

*"Now so it was that after three days they found Him in the temple, sitting in the midst of the teachers, both listening to them and asking them questions. And all who heard Him were astonished at His understanding and answers. So when they saw Him, they were amazed; And His mother said to Him, 'Son, why have you done this to us? Look, Your father and I have sought You anxiously. And He said to them, 'Why did you seek Me? Did you not know that I must be about My Father's business?' But they did not understand the statement which He spoke to them."*
Luke 2:46-49

■■■■■■■■■■■■■■■■■■■■■■■■■■■■■■■■■■■■■■■■■

Following Mary and Joseph's annual pilgrimage to Jerusalem for the Feast of the Passover, they discovered only one day into their return trip home that Jesus was nowhere to be found. They did what any parent of a twelve-year-old son would have done, and began to search diligently for Him. The Bible tells us that they started with their friends and relatives and eventually worked their way back to Jerusalem. It took three days before Mary and Joseph finally found Jesus, of all places, sitting calmly in the Temple with the Jewish Rabbis engaging in deep theological discussions.

It's no wonder Mary responded the way she did by asking Jesus how He could have done that to them, adding that, for three days, she and Joseph had been anxiously looking for Him. For any parent who has experienced the heart-pounding alarm that comes from even a few seconds in a store or a parking lot without seeing your child, you know the agony of such an experience. But *three days* would be nearly unbearable. I'm sure their sleep was light and troubled and they were probably exhausted mentally and physically by the time they found Jesus in the Temple.

Jesus' response to Mary that He needed to be doing God's work was something neither parent could understand. Luke 2:51-52 goes on to say, *"Then*

*He went down with them and came to Nazareth and was subject to them, but His mother kept all these things in her heart. And Jesus increased in wisdom and stature, and in favor with God and men."* The next 18 years of Jesus' life are veiled in silence, and it wouldn't be until the beginning of His public ministry that the Bible would lift that veil. Mary and Joseph were, no doubt, continually amazed at this gift of their son, announced by an angel, conceived by the Holy Spirit, and destined to change the course of humanity forever. They had the awesome privilege of being able to watch Him grow into the man that would one day hang on a cross for the sins of the world, which of course included their sins too.

From time to time, we may be aware of a feeling of separation from Jesus as we go about our daily lives. We may forget to pray, neglect Bible study and the things of God, and then a problem strikes and we look around to find that we've left Him behind. As a Christian, the cultivation of our relationship with Jesus is absolutely essential and anything less than a right relationship with Him will not satisfy. Then, as we search for Him in desperation, we're reminded that He is all we'll ever need and we just can't get to Him fast enough. I find it interesting that for three days He was hidden from Mary and Joseph, just as He was later hidden from the world for three days before He rose from the grave.

There are other times, also, when we may not see Jesus working in our lives and we may wonder why prayers aren't answered and periods of time pass without relief of our problems. Let me assure you that Jesus is always doing His Father's business. He may be silent, but He is always with you because He loves you and desires that you serve Him in obedience and love. Let's not forget either what Jesus was doing when they found Him. He was listening and answering questions that were most likely heavy theological ones. The Bible tells us that those around Him were overwhelmed by His understanding and wisdom. Jesus has the answers to your problems too. He wants to listen to what you tell Him and will answer in the most perfect way.

**What is God teaching me from today's devotional?**

# INTERCEDING IN FAITH

*"...since He always lives to make intercession for them."*
Hebrews 7:25b

Intercessory prayer is most commonly defined as a prayer to God on behalf of someone else. Prayers of intercession are found all throughout the Bible. Prophets interceded for the deliverance of the nation of Israel time and time again; everyone from David to Daniel to Paul were examples of those who pleaded on behalf of someone else for God's mercy and perfect will. Intercession doesn't mean that we can pray salvation on someone else because that is a personal decision, but it does mean that we can pray for God's intervening presence in the life of another.

Jesus is actively and continually interceding on our behalf. In fact, He's standing in the gap of the temptations and weaknesses into which we're most susceptible to falling. Romans 8:26-28, *"Likewise the Spirit also helps in our weaknesses. For we do not know what we should pray for as we ought, but the Spirit Himself makes intercession for us with groanings which cannot be uttered. Now He who searches the hearts knows what the mind of the Spirit is, because He makes intercession for the saints according to the will of God."* Who else but God can truly understand and know what is best for us, what we need most, and what the best direction for our life should be at any given time? Naturally, it stands to reason then that Jesus intercedes on our behalf for our good and His glory. Christ serves as the ultimate example of intercessory prayer. Hebrews 7:25b *"...since He always lives to make intercession for them."*

If you're a Christian, chances are pretty great you've been asked to pray for someone. Perhaps you see a situation where you know that prayer is needed. *Don't assume someone else is praying for the need.* You may be the only person aware of that particular situation in order that you might intercede on behalf of the person or situation. Be sure that your heart is pure before God, meaning that there is no unconfessed sin in your life, and then earnestly go to the Lord, standing in the gap for another's need. This is powerful spiritual warfare and you can expect that there will be resistance, but God will honor this genuine prayer. And by all means, if you tell someone you're going to pray for them, please do pray. I love it when someone reaches out to me to let me know that they've been praying for me. In fact, it encourages me to pray for others too.

Dietrich Bonhoeffer, that great Christian preacher and martyr of WWII under the Nazi regime, described intercessory prayer as *"(a) way of loving others when God's Spirit moves within us causing us to want to pray for others and giving us thoughts (ways) to do it."* When you feel Christ prompting you to pray for others, by all means respond to Him. Prayer changes things and people. Prayer matters and is powerful in ways that I don't think we may fully understand here on earth. Jesus took prayer so seriously that He actually *taught* us how to pray by giving us what we commonly call The Lord's Prayer.

Remember also that some of our prayers of intercession may go on for long periods of time. Don't despair! It's our job to respond to the Holy Spirit's prompting. We may only be planting a seed, but Chris is sovereign and His holy purpose will be done. I've personally experienced seasons of prayer that have taken years to see answered, but I trust and believe that God is always behind the scenes of those times working out His perfect will for both the person praying and the person being prayed for. Keep praying!

**What is God teaching me from today's devotional?**

# EACH & EVERY DAY

*"Blessed be the Lord, Who daily loads us with benefits, The God of our salvation!"*
Psalm 68:19

I find myself quite literally counting the days until a happy occasion, like a vacation or a holiday. I've found myself saying out loud some mornings, *"Well, only ___ more days until Christmas."* My son, in looking forward to his birthday, will ask me many times during the year, *"How many more days until I'm one year older?"* Sometimes I also end up counting the days until some not-so-pleasant situation, like a visit to the dentist or a tough meeting at work. We jokingly say that we live for Fridays and dread Mondays. It's human nature to remember with joy those happy days of our lives and struggle to let go of those days that brought sorrow or pain.

We are such creatures of habit, aren't we? Most of us get up at the same time each day, go through the same morning routine, drive the same route to work or school, associate with the same group of people, eat the same foods, and go to bed around the same time. There is a transparent comfort in familiarity, yet often the routine of things can become laborious if not mixed up. Despite the fact that we are given one day at a time, we worry about things years down the road, many of which will probably never happen. We are prone to let our imaginations run away from us every time we hear bad news or face uncertain circumstances and then we allow anxiety to push us further away from the day we're in until the present moment is completely ignored. Ask most people about what they spent their day doing, and, if truthfully told, they spent a lot of time unnecessarily worrying about events far off in the future.

The Lord's Prayer, that beautiful lesson on how we ought to pray, reminds that we are given "our daily bread". We should ask for (and expect) what we need for the day we're in presently. We also know that the Lord, *"daily bears our burdens"*, Psalm 68.19. We are warned against letting our worries and apprehensions get ahead of us. Matthew 6:34 tells us not to worry about tomorrow, but rather to focus on today. Time after time the Lord gives us assurance that He will never leave us and that He is guiding our steps daily. He doesn't want us to run ahead of Him, not even in our thought life.

I love Advent Calendars because there is a celebration of each day in December leading up to Christmas. An excitement builds as we anticipate Christmas Day, and yet we still give each day its own proper consideration. In the same way, we are supposed to be living our lives in expectant joy of the second coming of Christ while still finding joy in each day we're given. Truly, each and every day is a gift to be opened and treasured.

Good or bad, accept each day you're given, not mired in the past or fearful of the future. Enjoy today right alongside The Bread of Life, your daily bread! As the great Christian woman, writer, and Nazi death camp survivor, Corrie Ten Boom, said, "Worry does not empty tomorrow of its sorrow. It empties today of its strength." Go out in strength, TODAY.

**What is God teaching me from today's devotional?**

# DO I FIT IN?

*"Before I formed you in the womb I knew you; before you were born, I sanctified you...."*
Jeremiah 1:5a

"Fitting in" has been one of our struggles since we were first waiting to be picked for kickball on an elementary school playground. We so wanted the team captain to choose us because it meant we were liked, accepted, and valued. Later on we discovered that there were groups of people who represented some sort of security of belonging and we were either a part of that group or we weren't. We tried to copy models in magazines who we believed represented fashion and beauty and we desperately wanted to be part of the "in crowd". I can remember thinking I would die if I didn't get a snow white, imitation, rabbit fur coat in the sixth grade (back when that was the thing). I had seen a photo in a JC Penney catalog of a beautiful little girl wearing one and I guess I wanted to look like her. I didn't get one and I didn't die after all.

As we've gotten older, we may have joined various groups or clubs that promised some sort of identity. We hope and pray that after our teenage and young adult years the peer pressure of fitting in will all go away – and yet it doesn't. I would even argue that there's a little more peer pressure in my adult years than I personally experienced as a young woman. There's the pressure to be the perfect wife and mother, have the perfect career, stabilize everything around us for everyone around us, and still manage to find time for ourselves. It's an impossible dream because we weren't created to be all to all; we were created to rely on Jesus for our every need.

With so many forms of social media swirling around us we now see all the details of others' lives that had previously been hidden from our view. It's almost too easy to play the comparison game – (a game, by the way, where no one ever wins.) The Bible is clear when it says that comparing ourselves one to another is not wise. (II Corinthians 10:12) In other words, it's foolish to compare your life with someone else's. We can easily be deceived into believing that everyone else has a more attentive husband, nicer in-laws, more well-behaved kids, a prettier home, a newer vehicle, more friends, better health, more disposable income, a prettier face…the list goes on and on. If we could ever just be content with what God has entrusted us with we could genuinely experience true joy!

The most joyful women (and men) I know all have a common denominator; they are truly content with what they have and who they are in Christ. I've written so many times that Satan's oldest lie is that God is not enough for our needs. When we believe that we need to supplement God with *anything*, we are heading down the wrong path in a hurry. I have a little bookmark on my phone that says, "Mom (never enough) + God (infinitely enough) = Mom enough." For me it's a constant reminder that as a human being I will never have enough confidence, self-control, intelligence, or discernment on my own. I was born needing a Savior. With Him in control, I am then able to live this life to its fullest.

Let go of trying to be a part of "that group" or trying to look "that way" or trying to please "those people". Be yourself – the beautiful creation God intended to glorify Him. When your focus is on pleasing Christ through sold-out obedience to His Word, you <u>will</u> fit in perfectly to the plan He custom-designed for your life. I can promise you, based on the authority of God's Word, that, whether or not you even know it right now, you want to be in the center of His will. It is a place of safety, peace, and joy, no matter what circumstances swirl around you. You were not created to be on the outside looking in, but rather on the inside of God's perfect will positively influencing those who need Him.

**What is God teaching me from today's devotional?**

# VERY SCARY STRAWBERRY STEMS

*"Whenever I am afraid, I will trust in You."*
Psalm 56:3

The other night, as I was doing my routine walkthrough of the house in preparation for bedtime, I came across a scary sight in a semi-lit corner of our Den. Just as my hand was about to reach for the light switch, I saw three very large spiders on the table right beside where I was standing. Needless to say, it gave me quite a start and I jerked my hand back instinctively before I quickly ran to grab a flyswatter and a paper towel (necessary weapons where spiders are involved). When I returned to the room, I found that the spiders hadn't moved an inch. In fact, they turned out not to be spiders at all, rather just very scary-looking dehydrated strawberry stems from one of my son's early morning snacks. I laughed at myself for a moment, cleared them away, and went to bed thinking of the unfounded anxiety I'd just experienced.

Many things we encounter every day can appear to be frightening: we have an ache or a pain and we imagine the worst, our spouse is traveling and we imagine infidelity, our children are preoccupied and we begin to wonder if they really care about us at all, we have a hard week at work and we wonder if we should be polishing up our resume. These things, and so many more, tend to become exaggerated imaginations if left unchecked for too long. Before we know it, we've imagined the worst possible outcome or scenario and are causing ourselves additional worry and anxiety. We have become experts at trying, prematurely, to write the last chapter of our situation without taking God's will or plan into account. Often, and regrettably, we sit mired in our worry and never once truly pray about what is disturbing us.

Thankfully, none of us know what the future holds. What we do know is that God's Word tells us over and over again to trust Him with the unknown. Today's verse reminds us that anytime we're afraid, we should stop relying on our own strength and just completely trust in Christ. This is an act of the will and is a practiced response to the situations that cause us concern. Every time you have a thought that seems to nearly overwhelm you, say to yourself, *"This is a warning, but this may be wrong."* Then think through the reality of the situation (maybe even write it down) and then pray very specifically about it. Wait a little while and see if you feel the same way you did when the panic of it seemed like a wave crashing over you. It's amazing how time and a few deep breaths have the effect of changing our perspective from one of alarm to one of sensibility.

This story has an equally interesting ending. The next day, as I was telling my son about the scary strawberry stems, he looked at me with his wrinkled forehead, and said, *"Mama, if they had been spiders, it would still have been ok."* From the mouths of babes, right? He was absolutely accurate. Even *if* the scary thing had been a scary thing, Christ would still have been in control. Years ago, I experienced something that I thought was the very worst thing that could ever have happened, and it was horrible at the time, but God has used all the things that I thought I'd never live through for His glory and my good.

So today, whether you're facing real spiders (so-to-speak) or just scary-looking strawberry stems, please be reminded that God is watching over you and He wants you to trust Him completely. Any time you're afraid, run to Him and trust that He will take care of you because He *will*. He delights to be our refuge and our strength and we can know, for all time, that we have Christ as our secure hiding place.

**What is God teaching me from today's devotional?**

# HAVE YOU FORGOTTEN?

*"Do you not yet understand, or remember the five loaves of the five thousand and how many baskets you took up?"*
Matthew 16:9

How quickly we tend to forget! I'm one of those people terrible with remembering names but very good with faces. In fact, I have to make a real effort to remember names when introduced to someone because I'm often more interested in what they're saying than I am in their name. While we look at this type of forgetfulness in a lighthearted way, there is a type of forgetting that is very painful. Have you ever been ignored, left out, or passed over? It can be a hurtful experience. We're also often guilty of forgetting to thank God for all He has done in our lives because we fail to see Him in our day to day life. Your job is not your Provider; God is. Your bank account is not your Security; God is. Your healthy habits, careful planning, and hopes are all of our own making. God is ultimately in control.

In today's scripture passage the disciples have found themselves without food and their faith is growing weak. Christ has to remind them of the miracle He performed just a short time previously in feeding the five thousand people gathered to hear Him speak. How quickly their stomachs had digested their faith! I find it interesting that Jesus pointedly asked them if they *understood* and if they *remembered*. He went so far as to remind them that <u>they</u> were the ones who collected all that was left over. They were the ones who had witnessed the miracle first-hand and had, quite literally, held the evidence of the miracle in the baskets of leftovers they had gathered. They must have been amazed as they saw the food being supernaturally multiplied again and again right before their very eyes!

Regrettably, we're often no different than those doubting disciples. God answers prayer upon prayer in our lives, constantly provides for our well-being, and yet we grow anxious at the next crossroads in our life as if we've never had a prayer answered or never been the recipient of the grace of God. We think that God has a limited supply of good and we fear that perhaps we've met the quota allotted to us. I've been guilty of thinking that I don't deserve any more blessings or that one great big blessing must be all I'll ever receive. Sometimes it even seems that evil is winning and good is diminishing. How foolish to doubt, especially when God has been faithful so many times before.

In Malachi 3:10 we're told, *"Bring all the tithes into the storehouse, that there may be food in My house, and try Me now in this, says the Lord of hosts, if I will not open for you the windows of heaven and pour out for you a blessing until it overflows."* God is referring to tithing in this passage, but the picture of the way in which He blesses us is clear: it is overflowing, poured out, and drenching. His blessings are not the sort that just barely meet a need; His blessings completely saturate our needs.

If we stop to think of all the answers to prayer in our lives and all the miracles that we've witnessed, why do we put a period at the end of the sentence? Our greatest blessings are yet to come! Heaven is our eternal home and one day we'll share in the full experience of a glorified body and mind. Meanwhile, we are commanded to trust in Christ. Whatever crossroads of faith you may find yourself at today, listen to His words and remember. John 15:11, *"These things I have spoken to you, that My joy may remain in you, and that your joy may be full."* Sometimes Christ may seem to be hidden in the shadows, but He is always with you. Now go forward in peace, understanding and remembering all He has already done for you, protected you from, and promises to do in the future.

**What is God teaching me from today's devotional?**

# IMAGINARY FRIENDS

*"A friend loves at all times, and a brother is born for adversity."*
Proverbs 17:17

*"Greater love has no one than this, than to lay down one's life for his friends. You are My friends if you do whatever I command you. No longer do I call you servants, for a servant does not know what his master is doing; but I have called you friends, for all things that I heard from My Father I have made known to you."*
John 15:13

■■■■■■■■■■■■■■■■■■■■■■■■■■■■■■■■■■■■■■■■■

When I was a little girl, like so many other children, I had an imaginary friend. Of all things, her name was *So and So*. I can only imagine that at the ripe old age of four, I'd heard people refer to "so and so" when they couldn't remember a person's name and I'd chosen it as a suitable pick for a friend's name. For some reason, which will forever remain unknown, I adopted *So and So* as my special friend about whom no one else knew. She liked all the same things I liked, she went everywhere I went, and she was never too busy to talk. She stayed around for about a year until my brother was born, and then I was content to store her away in memory, since he then received all my attention and affection.

True friendships are precious and few, usually solidified by some sort of shared experience that unites the bond of hearts. I am blessed with some wonderful friends whom I know I can depend upon when I need them, but I'm also not around them all that often. In this season of my life, I'm busy caring for my family, working, and trying to fit a few extras into long weeks. Most of my friends are in the same boat. We all live very busy lives, filled full of things that try to rob us of the time that cultivating a friendship requires. Most families today are isolated by their own making; there's just simply not enough time, regrettably, to carve out time for friendships. It takes a real effort to make time for friendships.

I read the most interesting thing the other day in an article entitled, *Imaginary Friends*, by Eileen Kennedy-Moore, Ph.D., in Psychology Today. Ms.

Kennedy-Moore wrote (and I'm paraphrasing here) that even imaginary friends take time to develop. She wrote that children usually only develop those friendships in having unstructured time away from media, like television, phones, and other technology. What a lesson; even imaginary friendships take some effort to develop! Think for a moment about what the Bible says about friendship. Today's scriptures are but two in a long list of verses and passages dedicated to instruction and comment about true, genuine friendship. Friendships matter, but they absolutely have to be cultivated and cared for to be truly significant and successful. They can't be one-sided and they absolutely <u>must</u> be authentic. The quickest way to ruin a friendship is to betray it, but all friendships face tests of their endurance. The bottom line is that we desperately need friends in all seasons of life. True, none of us are perfect and we've all failed one another from time to time; however, a true friend never stays away too long or goes too long without checking in with the other person. Friendships require closeness.

    Finally, Jesus was the perfect example of a friend because He gave His life for us. How many of us would die for our friends? Jesus loves us when we choose unwisely, when we are grieving, when we are facing adversity, and at all other times. He loves us. Period. He is the truest friend you will ever have, so ask yourself how much time you've spent this week talking with Him in prayer, reading His love letter to us (the Bible), and telling others about what how much you love Him. Please don't take Him for granted or assume that your relationship with Him will grow just because you sit in a church service or say a rehearsed prayer over your food. The closer you draw to Him, the closer you'll be to your family and friends because the love He shows you will just naturally bubble over in your other relationships. Take a moment and think of a friendship you've been neglecting and then do something about it today. Most importantly, make sure your relationship with Christ isn't being ignored; He is the friend that sticks closer than a brother.

**What is God teaching me from today's devotional?**

# MANY, MANY THINGS

*"But the Lord answered her, 'Martha, Martha, you are getting worried and upset about too many things'."*
Luke 10:41

I have been deeply impressed recently by the passage of scripture found in Luke 10:38-42. This is the familiar story of Mary and Martha as they interacted with Jesus while He was a guest in their home. Martha was so frustrated that her sister, Mary, was just sitting with Jesus listening to Him speak, while Martha was trying to manage the household. Martha's frustration finally boiled over and she tried to get Jesus to move Mary to help her. I've read these verses countless times over the years, but only recently, during a time of prayer, did God really speak these words into my heart about my own life. Martha was distracted and worried about *many, many things*, certainly not just the house cleaning or the meal preparation. We often assume that Martha's only concern was that Mary wasn't doing her fair share of the cooking and cleaning, when actually Martha was most likely prone to worry and agonize about <u>many</u> things. It was probably an ongoing feeling of hers that she was doing it all while everyone else sat around doing things that weren't as important.

Jesus speaks to Martha in verse 42, *"Only one thing is important. Mary has chosen the right thing, and it will never be taken away from her."* Here Jesus reminds Martha (and all of us) that of all the things she's concerned about, only one thing truly matters: having a right relationship with Him and being attentive to His voice. I'm prone to worry too; in fact, there are times I can really get myself worked up into a major worry wart if I'm not careful. We worry about finances, our health, our jobs, our family members, what someone did or didn't say on social media, the future, and the list goes on and on… What God impressed upon me was that He wants me to keep my focus on Him, no matter what. Even if we're short of money, even if health fails, even if friends let you down, even as death comes to those we love, we are still told to trust Christ. The concrete assurance that Christ is always with us, and that He will work out all things for our good and His glory, is one thought that will defeat worry.

Tomorrow is a new day! No matter if it's a day full of blessings or discouragement, take a moment to ask God to renew your faith and trust in Him. Then move forward looking up. I remember something I learned during my sixth grade year at summer camp. The last night of camp, our counselors had us make a list of all the things we were worried about. We then took the list and threw it into a bonfire. This was to be symbolic of casting our fears away and starting life anew. Truth be told, my list was long even then as a twelve-year-old. Looking back at my diary from those years, I spent a lot of time worrying that I'd get appendicitis! It sounds silly now, but I knew someone who'd had appendicitis and it scared me to death for some reason. I knew that God was in control, but I was still clutching to anxiety and fear as if the worry gave me power over my circumstances.

When we continually release our worries to Him and refocus on the ONE THING that really matters, God is glorified. Remember, no matter what fears the enemy is whispering in your ear or convincing you that you can't live through, remember that we're not to fret over working out our own dilemmas. Be assured that Satan would love nothing more than for you to be an ineffective Christian, one so consumed with your own worries and concerns that there's no room for you to serve others or worship God. Christ wants you to hand Him your worries and then just rest in His presence. Jesus offers many, many things that are wonderful and life-changing. Cling to those good things and be blessed!

**What is God teaching me from today's devotional?**

# I'M LATE, I'M LATE, FOR A VERY IMPORTANT DATE

*"For I know the thoughts that I think toward you, says the Lord, thoughts of peace and not of evil, to give you a future and a hope."*
Jeremiah 29:11

■■■■■■■■■■■■■■■■■■■■■■■■■■■■■■■■■■■■■■

I was born a punctual person; a trait definitely inherited from my father. He and I are always on time, no matter what. Lateness is somewhat a pet peeve of mine because I make such a point of always being on time, and am usually even a bit early most of the time. I have to watch myself so that I don't go overboard with being this way; however, in our culture, promptness is a desirable attribute. In the keeping of our day-to-day schedules, it's important to the overall success of things that we try to be as punctual as possible. We often get aggravated by waiting at the grocery store, the doctor's office, a traffic light, and on the phone, yet we fail to keep the small appointments we make between friends, at church, or other obligations to which we're committed. We want others to be on time, but we often make excuses for ourselves.

In the story of Alice in Wonderland, you may recall the White Rabbit running around and fretting because he was perpetually late for his appointments. The Disney movie made his line famous, *"I'm late, I'm late, for a very important date."* We're no different in some ways as we run about panicked by the obligations and stresses that demand our presence. Even if you're not the most punctual person, it's easy to become frustrated when the timing in your life seems wrong. We resent having to wait because it feels like a disruption to our lives. After all, we have so much to do, right? Sometimes we're most frustrated with God's timing and we may ask questions like, "Why isn't God on time?" "Doesn't He know my need? "When will God ever intervene?" Without intending to, we often act as if God is working for us and that He has an obligation to do things according to our calendar.

I can't help but think of the story in John 11 where Lazarus has died and Mary runs to Jesus to question him in verse 35. She says, "*. . . if you had been here, my brother wouldn't have died."* The implication is that if Jesus had been on time, Lazarus would not have died. In verse 37, some of those in the crowd that day agreed with Mary by saying, *"Could not this man, which opened the eyes of the blind, have caused that even this man should not have died?"* We know the story of how Jesus called for Lazarus and he was raised from the dead. Jesus could very well have prevented Lazarus' death and spared Mary and Martha the grief they had felt for days. Verse 45 gives us a clue as to the timing and what it meant, *"Then many of the Jews which came to Mary, and had seen the things which Jesus did, believed on him."* Had Lazarus not died and then been raised, many may not have believed. It took something horrible for something beautiful to come of it.

The next time you're tempted to question God's timing, be reminded that His timing is always perfect. His ways are always best. His perspective is eternity, and He is watching over you. He will never be too early or too late. As today's verse in Jeremiah reminds us, the Lord has us on His mind and has a definite plan for our life. Not just any plan, His plan is for a hopeful future, one specially and intentionally designed by Him for us. Let this thought comfort you the next time you're early or late: The God of the universe is always on time.

**What is God teaching me from today's devotional?**

# A TIME TO HEAL

*"To everything there is a season, A time for every purpose under heaven."… "A time to heal."*
Ecclesiastes 3:1, 3b

The healing process can sometimes take a lot longer than we'd like. Whether it be a broken bone, a broken spirit, or a broken relationship, the course of healing is one that varies by individual and circumstance. There is no formula or precise schedule for the journey it takes one to go from the valley to the mountaintop, and the Bible gives us many examples of those for whom a trial or struggle took a long while. Think of Hannah, Sarah, Joseph, David, Habakkuk, and many others all throughout God's Word who had to walk slowly through the corridors of waiting.

Our scripture verses today tell us that there is a definite time and season for everything, including healing. The Wycliffe Bible Commentary, referring to this passage of scripture, beautifully states, *"Everything in nature and in human life is under a set scheme. There is a season (an appointed period) and a time (a predetermined occurrence) for all that takes place under the sun. Seeming chance events are all part of a huge plan."* There is nothing that happens in our lives which escapes God's notice and isn't divinely a part of His plan for us.

We are often guilty of expecting others to get better quickly and then stay better because it hurts us to see others hurting, especially those we love. We can be insensitive to the time that it takes to fully recover, and the person we're often most impatient with is the one we see in the mirror. I think what we're most uncomfortable with is the fact that it <u>does</u> take time. We'd much rather quickly and totally eradicate the problem so that the course of healing didn't have to take so long. Even with medicine and attention from specialists, we often have to take a more gradual route toward wellness than we would prefer and that can be a frustrating experience.

Healing is a season all its own. It can be excruciatingly painful to have to endure the days in which healing doesn't seem to come and setbacks seem to take the place of progress. We can begin to wonder if God is even listening to our prayers or if He cares at all. These times of vulnerability and feeling fragile are the times we need to be on guard against believing anything that isn't the truth about our situation. Satan would love to whisper in your ear that God is not really good after all because He's not answering your prayers on your timetable. The truth is rock-solid, however. God does love you. He does care about you. He has a plan that may not be apparent to you at this time, but He will work out all things for your good and His glory – that's a promise, but it's in His time.

So whatever you're going through right now, whether it be a short season of trial or a long, seemingly unending season of healing, I pray that you will be comforted in the fact that you don't have to be in a hurry. Allow God to heal your heart, your body, and your mind (or those you love and are concerned about) in His time. Realize that it may take a while and that's perfectly ok. Bask in the sunshine and the shadows of His love for you as you rest in Him. Remember in John chapter 4 when He confronted the woman at the well; Jesus was sitting at the well, calm and in control. Remember Jesus on the ship during the storm; He was asleep. He isn't anxious about our futures and we don't need to be either. Relax as you heal; Christ is there with you.


**What is God teaching me from today's devotional?**

# WHEN AN APOLOGY IS DUE

*"And forgive us our debts, as we forgive our debtors."*
Matthew 6:12

Stop for a second right now and ask yourself this question: *"Is there anyone who owes me an apology?"* How about this question: *"Do I owe anyone an apology?"* Sometimes a sincere apology is all that would be necessary to mend a relationship and bring harmony back into a given situation. In our homes and workplaces, there are times when a genuine apology is absolutely the *only* way to begin to fix the problem.

Proverbs is full of great counsel for daily living. In Proverbs 28:13, we're told, *"He who covers his sins will not prosper, but whoever confesses and forsakes them will have mercy."* We often get so busy in our everyday tasks that we develop tunnel vision, unable to see how our actions or inactions affect those around us. Some common examples might include snapping at a family member or co-worker, always being too busy to listen, half-listening, gossiping about something you know nothing about, an 'I could have done it better' attitude, insincere flattery, talking over someone, or having to be right all the time. The list could go on and on. Pray and ask the Holy Spirit to show you the areas you need to improve upon.

When you recognize an apology that is due, by all means do it quickly. The sooner you ask for forgiveness the better. Satan loves for us to harbor bitterness because that bitterness will soon become a poison that destroys your effectiveness as a Believer. Then learn to face the consequences of what you've done. Not everyone whose apology you ask for will carry on as if nothing happened. There may be hurt that will follow for a while, but part of doing the honorable thing is to humbly accept the consequences. Pride has to take the back seat as we acknowledge our wrongdoing both to God and to others.

What about the apology that never comes? How does a Christian respond to this? We're to respond like Christ. He forgave even in the face of betrayal, persecution, and finally death. Like most people, there are apologies that I feel I'll likely never receive. We *must* hand those things over to God. Only He has the capacity to handle these situations in the best way. I would be remiss to not add that an apology can't take back the hurt that was done, but a truly genuine asking of forgiveness is the first step to reconciliation.

Lastly, I want to share a quoted prayer that I read a while back. I think it brings all of this into focus.

*"I offer up unto Thee my prayers and intercessions, for those especially who have in any matter hurt, grieved, or found fault with me, or who have done me any damage or displeasure. For all those also whom, at any time, I have vexed, troubled, burdened and scandalized, by words or deeds, knowingly or in ignorance: that Thou wouldst grant us all equally pardon for our sins, and for our offences against each other. Amen."*
~Thomas A. Kempis


**What is God teaching me from today's devotional?**

# REST BESIDE THE WEARY ROAD

*"...Peace, peace to him who is far off and to him who is near, says the Lord."*
Isaiah 57:19b

I love the Christmas season, with all the expectations and anticipations that symbolize that most wonderful time of the year. Nothing quite ignites the Christmas spirit within me like singing Christmas carols while playing them on my old, upright piano. I particularly love to sing every verse because most have stirringly beautiful words of encouragement embedded in the third or fourth stanzas. Just recently I sat down to play the classic carol, *It Came Upon The Midnight Clear*, and noticed the oft-hidden third stanza. It reads, *And ye, beneath life's crushing load/ Whose forms are bending low,/ Who toil along the climbing way/ With painful steps and slow,/ Look now! For glad and golden hours/ Come swiftly on the wing;/ O rest beside the weary road,/ And hear the angels sing.*

Written in 1849 by Edmund H. Sears, the carol has come under scrutiny from time to time because it doesn't directly mention the word Jesus or Christ; however it does mention "Heaven's all gracious King." Regardless of any controversy, the Christian church has incorporated this carol into Christmas celebrations for well over 100 years. When I stopped to read and re-read stanza three, I was struck by the significance of the words and what many around the world are feeling. I hope not, but you may feel that you're carrying the weight of the world on your shoulders and that your steps forward are painful. Whether personally, as a family, or as a nation, we all have burdens to bear and they don't just go away in December. The beautiful words inside this Christmas carol remind us that there is a rest beside the weary road of life. That rest is Jesus. He calls us to Himself and His rest is not a vacation, a yoga mat, a self-help book, or our best attempts at turning over a new leaf. He is the only One Who can provide us the soul rest we so desperately need. Matthew 11:28-30, *"Come to Me, all you who labor and are heavy laden, and I will give you rest. Take My yoke upon you and learn from Me, for I am gentle and lowly in heart, and you will find rest for your souls. For My yoke is easy an My burden is light."*

I've walked down many weary roads in my lifetime and I've observed others on that same pathway, struggling at times just to keep moving forward. Life can be incredibly tough at times, but I'm so thankful that there is always the option of stopping for a while. Sometimes we're burning the candle at both ends and sometimes the candle seems to be burning us. Maybe it's a commitment you need to let go of for a time, or perhaps you need to let go of your own requirements of perfectionism. Whatever you need to release in order to focus on what really matters, I hope you will allow yourself to rest beside whatever weary road down which you may be walking.

Remember that all our hard work and struggling is but for a time anyway. Won't you try to allow yourself to set aside the burdens, no matter how difficult, and allow Christ to carry them for you? He came to earth as a baby so that He could die on the cross for our sins. His resurrection is as much a part of Christmas as His birth is a part of Easter; His whole life was a gift to us. Whether it's the Christmas season or any other season of the year, just slow down and allow yourself a time for rest, recovery, and reflection as you seek to honor Him with your life. You will find that Jesus will be right beside you where you rest as sure as He will be beside you when you pick up your journey. You are never alone.

**What is God teaching me from today's devotional?**

# BIG DREAMS IN ORDINARY PLACES

*"Behold, I am the LORD, the God of all flesh. Is anything too hard for me?"*
Jeremiah 32:37

▪▪▪▪▪▪▪▪▪▪▪▪▪▪▪▪▪▪▪▪▪▪▪▪▪▪▪▪▪▪▪▪▪▪▪▪▪▪▪▪▪▪▪▪▪

World-famous mystery writer, Agatha Christie, is credited with saying, "The best time to plan a book is while you're doing the dishes." It might be hard to imagine Agatha Christie doing dishes at all, much less planning books while doing so. Most of the photographs of her show us an elderly woman with razor-sharp eyes and a knowing look seated in a chair with a book in her hand, but Agatha Christie actually had a fascinating life, complete with adventure in far-away lands and even a mysterious period of time in her own life in which she went missing. If you like such things, her autobiography is one of the best I've ever read. Other writers chose ordinary ways to clear their minds and think of the future. Charles Dickens, for instance, infamously took long, night walks through London to plan his books.

I'm sure no fly on the wall would have observed Agatha Christie washing dishes and been able to envision the wildly successful career she would go on to achieve. Likewise, I daresay Charles Dickens went largely unnoticed in the early days, hidden away in the London fog, passing under gas-lit lamps at night, with his mind ablaze planning <u>A Christmas Carol,</u> a book that would go on to change the world's look at injustice and greed in the form of Scrooge.

Just because you're in a remote place, doesn't mean you can't dream big and also achieve those dreams! You may feel hidden away in a home with small children, buried under laundry, dirty dishes, and not a lot of money to stretch. You may be in a job that brings you little joy and yet you dream of the day when you can really use your natural abilities and strengths to spread your wings and fly. You may be at a point where you feel you're too old, too weak, or too insignificant to even have a dream. You may look behind you and see a string of broken dreams and feel that it's just not worth trying again. You are wrong! God says in today's verse that nothing is too hard for Him because He can help us achieve things that others would laugh at as impossible.

Whatever you're dreaming about, I want to ask you one question: Are you also praying about it? Have you handed it to Jesus to ask Him to help make that dream a reality, or are you just wishing that things would change and your dream would come true? If I've learned anything over the past two years, it is that dreams take a lot of work to see through to fruition. Most big dreams involve setbacks, disappointments, and struggles that require an equal or greater measure of determination, resilience, and faith. God places within each of our hearts certain desires that He wants to see bloom out in our lives because, rightly recognized, He is the giver of the dream and also the giver of the dream come true.

There are countless stories of people who saw their dreams become a reality because they didn't give up when times were hard or when others were telling them it would never happen. God delights in working miracles in situations where all hope appears to be lost. If your dream is committed to Christ and you're working toward seeing it fulfilled, the result rests with God alone, not other people. Nothing is too hard for Him. I pray that whatever ordinary place you're in right now, perhaps feeling that no one knows or cares, remember that God often uses quiet, obscure places to do His most magnificent preparations for greatness.

**What is God teaching me from today's devotional?**

# COVETOUSNESS AND THE USE OF THE COMMA

*"Let your conduct be without covetousness; be content with such things as you have. For He Himself has said, "I will never leave you nor forsake you." So we may boldly say: The Lord is my helper; I will not fear. What can man do to me?"*
Hebrews 13:5-6

▪▪▪▪▪▪▪▪▪▪▪▪▪▪▪▪▪▪▪▪▪▪▪▪▪▪▪▪▪▪▪▪▪▪▪▪▪▪▪▪▪▪▪

To covet, according to Webster's dictionary, means, *"to have a strong desire for something which belongs to another"*, and is also well-described as having a selfish, uncontrolled wish for something that isn't yours. The comma is the little punctuation mark that separates ideas within a sentence. You may be wondering what the correlation could possibly be between covetousness and a comma. The relationship between the two exists *in the pause* that separates two thoughts. For instance, we can go to a museum and truly admire a painting for its aesthetic beauty, BUT our appreciation for it takes a pause and is tested against what we know is right. It wouldn't be right for us to admire it, wish it was ours, and then attempt to take it from the museum. So while the feelings that priceless art, in this example, bring to the surface within us is tempered so that we wouldn't actually try to take it for our own. Covetousness is the subject of the tenth commandment mentioned in the Ten Commandments (see Exodus 20:17). This commandment involved the various shades of greed that take place first in the mind. God wants us to avoid the very thoughts that lead to sinful results.

We rarely ever use the word "covet" in today's vocabulary. Instead we use words like desire, want, crave, or long for, but it's subtly woven through our thoughts as things we "out to have" or even "deserve". When covetous thoughts take root in our minds and hearts, it's very ugly. If we are exercising our thoughts toward selfish longing for something that isn't ours and isn't meant to be ours, then we need to bring it before God in true repentance and confession. God already knows our hearts, and He will forgive and help us to control any selfish desires. Doesn't this sound like the first lie put to mankind? Satan tempted Eve with the idea that God was not good, and that the fruit she was told to avoid was really something God was selfishly withholding from her. We don't know how long it took for her to roll the idea around in her mind, but she eventually yielded to her greedy desire and sinned.

I think also that many of us covet something we *think* someone else has, as opposed to what they *actually* have. We see the surface in most cases – the social media profile, the Sunday morning version, or the "I'm-on-my-best-behavior" routine and we accept that as truth. So that the very thing we think we want is actually a mirage. Think also about how many times you've experienced buyer's remorse after having purchased something you thought you couldn't live without, only to be let down by the reality of it.

We have a choice every single day to either harbor selfish longings or to be submissive, obedient children of God. Ask yourself a few quick questions: Do you covet someone else's talent or special ability? Do you covet another person's husband? Do you covet another person's possessions? Do you covet another person's professional success? Insert the comma right now and surrender those feelings to Christ. Choose today to tell yourself the truth and focus on all you do have in Christ, free from any desire for something that isn't yours. After all, Christ is the only One Who can give your heart the things for which it longs, and the things it truly needs.

**What is God teaching me from today's devotional?**

# WHY DID THE TURKEY CROSS THE ROAD?

*"A merry heart does good, like medicine, but a broken spirit dries the bones."*
Psalm 17:22

I had an unusual experience last year. It was early one cold morning on my way to work, and I was lost in deep thought about the day ahead. As I was mentally running through my list of appointments to keep and decisions to be made, I began to feel a sense of anxiety creeping over me as I contemplated just how I was going to get it all done. Right about that time, while sitting at a familiar stoplight, I began to see people in cars around me rolling down windows and snapping photos. What I saw next surprised me! A family of five or six turkeys was slowly making their way across the busy intersection, right along with some (human) pedestrians. All around me, in cars and at a bus stop, people were smiling and laughing. The traffic light changed two or three times before the turkeys made it from one side of the street to the other, but the drivers on both sides of the light waited patiently, apparently happy to have had such an unexpectedly lighthearted disruption to their morning commute.

I love to laugh, and I love being around people who also love to laugh! Most of the time, I find that I'm laughing at myself ☺ There are several people in my life who I know I can count on when I need a pick-me-up because they understand, like the writer of today's Scripture passage, that laughter is good like medicine. Truly, a cheerful, contented disposition is a strong force against negativity, but to laugh is a solution to so many problems. A person with a merry heart has the ability to see past today's troubles into tomorrow's promises while not taking themselves too seriously.

The unpredictable experience of seeing those turkeys crossing the road made me think about how much joy and humor is all around us if we'd only open our eyes to see it. Unfortunately, we're often so swept up in our own schedules and plans that we miss out on some really fun moments. A great deal of our stress and anxiety can be lifted by a hearty laugh or a genuine smile. I encourage you today to look at the humor, the happiness, and the lightheartedness that is all around you as a gift from God. He can replace your worry and stress with smiles and laughter when you let go of feeling that you have to control every outcome. Of course there are days that feel like a different force of gravity and seriousness are demanded, but joy can be found even in the most trying of situations.

Try a sunnier approach to the demand right ahead of you, no matter how stressful or how large it looms in your anticipation of it. As you see a nerve-wracking day approaching, allow yourself to laugh. Think of the quirky imperfections of your family, the funny moments that occur at work, the silly antics of those around you, and especially yourself. Because Christ came, we can have real, genuine joy. Have you ever thought that one way to honor Him might be to show others, often through laughter, just how happy you are in this life? When others see that you're not caving under pressure but are instead laughing in spite of it, you can point the credit back to Jesus as the source of real gladness.

So, why did the turkey cross the road? I think it was to remind me that, in the midst of what felt like overwhelming responsibilities and demands, unanticipated joy can break through anywhere, and often in the most amazing ways. I'm also glad that I got to witness the situation first hand because it has left a happy memory behind that serves as a reminder to be on the lookout for the next unexpected, lighthearted moment. I pray that laughter will be the medicine to cure what's ailing you today!

**What is God teaching me from today's devotional?**

# MUSIC IN THE STORM

*"The Lord will command His lovingkindness in the daytime; and His song will be with me in the night, a prayer to the God of my life."*
Psalm 42:8

The wind was so strong one night recently, that the next morning revealed several downed tree limbs and power lines. All over our area, and on the local news and weather stations, people were talking about the wild winds that had whipped through the mountains of Western North Carolina. While not always so severe, the mountains generally have a breeze blowing somewhere. Since childhood, one of my very favorite sounds has been that of the wind whistling through the trees. Especially at night, I've always felt comforted by the indescribable and powerful sound of the wind, one of God's most unique creations. On the night the wind was so strong, I was in bed, wide awake, thinking about the events of the day ahead. I had a lot on my mind and not all of it was positive. My thoughts, however, were interrupted by the slightest hint of a beautiful sound; it was the wind chime on our porch just chiming away. A housewarming gift from some good friends of ours, I'd often sat on the porch and relaxed to its gentle tune, but this night was different; the wind chime was being knocked about by the violent wind. The more I concentrated on the sound of the chimes, the sound of the wind seemed to become all that more beautiful.

I thought of Psalm 42:8 and remembered that God tells us He will provide for us a song in the night. No matter how bleak or dreary the outlook may *feel*, we can be assured that God is with us when we need Him the most. The song of the wind chime during the day, barely moved by a gentle breeze, is peaceful and relaxing, but the song of the chimes when battered by fierce wind and rain, is louder and even more reassuring. So then, what is the song that God gives? I believe He reminds us of the day prior, the moment we're in, and the days ahead. Just as Hebrews 13:8 says, *"Jesus Christ is the same yesterday and today and forever."* He never changes and we can rest in the reassurance that He is in control. He is watching over us and can calm our fears and anxieties. Our 'song' is the remembrance of His promises and answered prayers. The song is also just praise to Him for Who He is as Lord of all. The ultimate song is that of future promises yet to be fulfilled – a life with Him forever.

I hope that the winds blowing in your life right now are only gentle breezes, but if life is coming at you in blistering gusts of unsteadying uncertainty, I pray you will grasp hold of Christ as your anchor in the storm. Charles Spurgeon wrote a famous sermon in the late 1800's entitled, *Songs in The Night*. One of the now-famous passages from that sermon sums up this beautiful subject. Spurgeon wrote, *"It is not love to Christ to praise Him while everybody else praises Him; to walk arm in arm with Him when He has the crown on His head is no great deed, but to walk with Christ in rags is something. To believe in Christ when He is shrouded in darkness, to stick close to the Savior when all those around you mock Him and forsake Him – that is true faith. They who sing a song to Christ in the night, sings the best song in the entire world; for they sing from the heart."* I pray we all have the courage to live for Him in the day and to not doubt or grow weary in the dark seasons. Morning will surely come and may we all be encouraged by the music we heard and the song we sang in the night.

**What is God teaching me from today's devotional?**

# QUIET!

*"Then He arose and rebuked the wind, and said to the sea,' Peace, be still!' And the wind ceased and there was a great calm."*
Mark 4:39

▪▪▪▪▪▪▪▪▪▪▪▪▪▪▪▪▪▪▪▪▪▪▪▪▪▪▪▪▪▪▪▪▪▪▪▪▪▪▪▪

Isn't it ironic that we often <u>yell</u>, *Quiet!*, when the last thing we want is more noise? Just the other day I was with my son at an event with lots of other children his age. The group of kids was having a great time, but their voices were increasingly becoming louder and louder. The adult in charge first called out, and then loudly yelled out to get their attention. Soon all the children were back to using their inside voices. All they needed was a reminder that they were getting out of control, but they couldn't hear the message for their own commotion.

We are like those children in many instances: our lives have become more and more chaotic, our internal voices drown out God's still, small voice, and before long we are in a tailspin of our own making. It takes the authoritative voice of our Shepherd to draw us back to Him. Do you remember how Jesus spoke to the storm out on the Sea of Galilee? He had one simple command, *"Peace, be still."* The Bible says that the wind and the waves obeyed Him, and His disciples were amazed. In the same way, He still speaks peace into hearts that are overburdened, overextended, and out of control. When we are at peace, it is a testimony to others of our relationship with Christ, but it's an even louder message when we're at peace inside a stormy situation.

Thankfully, Jesus gives us the antidote to this hurried state of life. He tells us in Psalm 46:10, *"Be still, and know that I am God."* We are told to quiet ourselves and listen for His voice. It's so easy to live from one appointment to the next, one day to the other, one set of responsibilities to the next, without taking time to be still and prayerfully consider which direction God would have us go.  Think about God's command to honor the Sabbath day and keep it holy.  He means for us to come apart one day each week to rest and be restored.  All too often, many people think this only means church attendance, and then they zoom off to tackle the same types of things they do any other day of the week.  More and more, many professing Christians see worship on Sundays as an option – after all, they're just so busy.  We can easily justify the demands of our lives as the reason for not getting together with friends, not volunteering where needed, and many other things.

If we're going to have real peace and quiet in our lives, we <u>must</u> stop and rest.  We will be better for it and our families will be also.  Having a day of quiet equips us for the week ahead; we can plan and prepare, refuel and recharge, and rest our bodies for the work ahead.  We need the retreat of a day set apart so that our minds can rest also.  The more I plan to quiet myself, the better I feel.  There is enough clamoring for our attention, so why not intentionally try to create a space of rest each Sunday?  Honor the Lord with worship in church and let that set the tone for your day of seeking repose in Him.  Maybe you just need to change the way you prioritize Sundays, but I promise it will do you tremendous good.

For a few weeks, try being very deliberate in protecting Sunday from anything other than church attendance and time with your family.  It will take some planning so that you won't need to go to the grocery store or the gas station or wherever else, but it can be done.  Create some time on Sunday afternoon or evening that is quiet time for each person in your home so that everyone knows that time is for that person.  I have done this and it is amazing how much better the week ahead will flow just by stopping on Sunday.  After all, God intended for us to have a day of rest and His plan is always perfect.

**What is God teaching me from today's devotional?**

# A PICTURE PERFECT FAMILY

*"For your Maker is your husband, The Lord of hosts is His name..."*
Isaiah 54:5a
*"When my father and my mother forsake me, Then the Lord will take care of me.""*
Psalm 27:10

━━━━━━━━━━━━━━━━━━━━━━━━━━━━━━━━━━

    Norman Rockwell is my very favorite American artist; his paintings capture life in such a unique and profound way. His series of oil paintings from 1943, called the *Four Freedoms*, were inspired by Franklin D. Roosevelt's 1941 State of the Union address, also referred to as the Four Freedoms Speech. Norman Rockwell brilliantly painted *Freedom of Speech, Freedom of Worship, Freedom from Want, and Freedom from Fear*. If you're unfamiliar with these significant works of art, I encourage you to seek them out.

    *Freedom from Want*, in particular, has become part of the American story due its iconic representation of the ideal holiday family get-together. It didn't take long for the painting to became associated with Thanksgiving and was soon burned into the American psyche as what we should all seek to attain. The faces around the table in the painting are actually friends of Rockwell's whom he painted separately and then pulled together to create his famous white on white oil painting.

    Even today, the painting's impact endures as the dream many of us wish we could capture and copy. The problem is, however, that most family gatherings aren't ones in which so many generations are gathered around a crisp white tablecloth about to devour a perfectly-prepared turkey with our newly-polished silver. Many of our gatherings have chairs that sit empty due to death, divorce, estrangement, or a multitude of other reasons that keep family members apart from one another. Whatever the makeup of your family gatherings, I pray that you will remember what the Bible tells us. In the scripture passages I've listed today, notice how God steps in as husband to the woman without a husband, father to the orphan and abandoned, and friend to all of us who know Him.

I realize the awful hurt and pain when our families are distanced from us for any reason. Perhaps there isn't a physical distance, just more of a level of discomfort or unresolved pain. Maybe you see one another, but can never get to the real core of the problems that have taken deep roots. There's nothing worse than the proverbial elephant in the room – a problem so large and painful, yet always going unaddressed. I encourage you to fervently pray about this and then try your best to find meaningful, respectful ways to reach resolution. If you've tried and feel you've gotten nowhere, keep praying! Let God do what God does best, which is to work miracles in the hardest to reach places with what seems to be the hardest to reach people.

Lastly, when we think about the perfect family, let's not get lost in the tablecloth or the food (so to speak). I think one reason people become so concerned about their "things" being just-so is because their relationships are not. The next time you're at a family gathering, find causes to be thankful. Be grateful for the time you have with the ones you have time with, and enjoy all the blessings on your table at that moment. Remember, one day we'll have a meal like none we've ever had. Revelation 9:6-9 describes the marriage supper of the Lamb, in which Christ and His church come together to celebrate. Can you even imagine what that will be like? That is one gathering that really will be perfect!

**What is God teaching me from today's devotional?**

# THE "ER" DILEMMA

*"...for I have learned, in whatever state I am, to be content."*
Philippians 4:11b

Since the time we were in elementary school, two little letters have caused us a lot of unnecessary grief and anxiety. The two letters are *"e-r"* and they represent the inaccurate perception that someone else is somehow succeeding where we're left lacking. Allow me to explain: *She's prettier than me. Their home is nicer than ours. She's thinner than me. Her car is newer than mine. Her job is higher up the career ladder than mine. Their kids are faster learners than mine. Her husband is nicer than mine.* Many a pity party over the years has been borne of these kinds of comparisons.

We begin equating ourselves to others just as soon as we buy into the notion that success, wealth, beauty, and pleasure are actually attainable goals. However, when is enough success really enough? How much money is enough? When are the expectations of you at work ever really fulfilled? When is beauty ever portrayed as something that can actually be achieved? By the world's standards, the answer is a resounding, *never.* Just as soon as you've paid off one debt, the temptation is to take on another. Just as quickly as you have a great hairstyle or wardrobe, the temptation is to update it. Just when you're sure that you have everything to make your life comfortable and pleasurable, something new comes along that you feel you just have to have. After all, the latest, greatest thing could really change your life for the better, right? If you just work a little harder or receive a little more praise, life will be great, right? It was rightly said that the enemy of good is better, and the enemy of enough is more. So, why then are we chasing the wind when it comes to these sorts of things?

There's nothing wrong with bettering ourselves or with staying current, but when we're ruled by the pressure to do so, there's a problem. When the pursuit of things or praise outpaces our pursuit of God, we enter into an impossible swirl. The Bible talks a lot about contentment and humility. In today's passage of scripture, we see that contentment is possible, but it's a learned response. At the root of all contentment is contentment with Who God is. We can never be exhaustively content with anything or anyone unless we've first come to a place of utter contentment in Christ. When we're resting in a contented place with Him (meaning that He's all we're depending upon for our joy), we will find that everything else will line up in order of importance behind Him. He will be our primary focus, not success or material things.

Ask yourself right now whether or not you believe God is both good and sovereign. He is both. He is overwhelmingly good and He is utterly sovereign. His will is the only perfect one and it will stand the test of all time. Thank Him for what He has allowed in your life and for what He has disallowed. The next time you're tempted to allow comparisons to others get you down, remember that God never intended for us to live in anyone's shadow, but His. Let Him shadow you with the protective cover of His love and acceptance in a way that blocks out any other temptation or influence to seek anything other than Him for your happiness.

**What is God teaching me from today's devotional?**

# I NEED A HAND

*"Come to Me, all you who labor and are heavy laden, and I will give you rest."*
Matthew 11:28

*"...I will uphold you with My righteous right hand."*
Isaiah 41:10b

⋯⋯⋯⋯⋯⋯⋯⋯⋯⋯⋯⋯⋯⋯⋯⋯⋯⋯⋯⋯⋯⋯⋯⋯⋯⋯

    As hard as it is for me to do, from time to time I have to ask for help. This shouldn't be such a struggle, but I find that it's very difficult for me to admit to others that I need some type of assistance. It's twice as hard for me to admit to myself that I can't manage everything in my life without some help now and then. Last winter I saw this concept put into concrete form as my son and I went sledding down an icy hill on a snow day. My little boy had gone zipping down the frozen slope and landed on a patch of ice. As I hurried down the hill toward him, I could see that his shoes were gaining no traction and he was absolutely unable to stand, much less walk, on the ice. No matter how hard he struggled, he was getting nowhere fast. Just before I got to him, he cried out, *"Mommy, if you don't give me your hand I'll be slipping around here forever and ever!"*

    My son's statement carried with it a profound truth about how we often end up in need and in limbo. Sometimes we are all just slipping around, gaining no traction, unable to move, and in desperate need of a hand to rescue us out of a given situation. I'm so thankful that, as Christians, Jesus stands ready to help us any time we call on Him. The Scriptures are full of reminders and admonitions to come to Him and to trust in His ability to lift us out of a situation beyond our control. I'm so grateful that His loving and powerful hand is extended and always ready to help.

    As a Christian community, we're also called to lift each other up. I've often heard people pray that the Lord would multiply our joys and divide our sorrows. Sorrows are usually divided when others are helping to lift us up.

Indeed, there are times when we all need encouragement and inspiration, and sometimes, as hard as it may be, we have to _ask_ for it. There have been a few times recently when I've had to rely upon others and it has reminded me of how much more I should be readily available to those around me.

Several years ago, after a major surgery, several women in my church came one day and cleaned my house from top to bottom. They even cleaned walls, baseboards, and my ceiling fans! It was a beautiful picture of a true servant's heart. None of us can read minds, but we can be sensitive to the obvious needs around us. We can also let others know that we're there for them, as a safe place, if they need us. Sometimes we may be called to react in an anonymous way, providing support from a distance, and then other times we may be needed to organize and lead others to action for a special cause.

If today you feel like my son did on that icy patch of ground, unable to find your footing, please don't stay there. Reach out to Christ and then reach out to others. I've found that when I've shared a prayer request or a need with those who really care about me, the love and concern has been tremendous. We weren't made to live this life all to ourselves, but rather to experience it with others – through the good days and the harder days as well.

**What is God teaching me from today's devotional?**

# ANOTHER PERSPECTIVE ON THE NATIVITY SCENE

*"The thief does not come except to steal, and to kill, and to destroy. I have come that they may have life, and that they may have it more abundantly."*
John 10:10

The Christmas story is an important story any time of the year, yet I've been guilty at times of reading that familiar narrative in a rehearsed way. Many of us know Luke chapter two by heart, or at least with a little prompting could quote several verses with no trouble. After all, it's so familiar, right? The angel Gabriel, Mary, Joseph, no room at the inn, the manger, the shepherds, the chorus of angels...and so it goes. In my devotional time a while back I prayed and asked the Lord to show me things about this passage of scripture that I hadn't noticed before. If you want to see a prayer answered in a hurry, pray that way!

We know from Matthew chapter two that when the wise men came to Jerusalem in search of the King of the Jews, they were quickly intercepted by Herod. Herod was highly interested in their plight and sought to lay a trap for them. He asked that when they did find the young child to please let him know so that he could go and worship him. Of course we all know that Herod only wanted to kill anyone he perceived as a threat to his position. God's providential protection was overshadowing Jesus, and so the wise men were warned in a dream to return another way and not go back to Herod with news of Jesus. Joseph was also warned in a dream to take Mary and Jesus and flee into Egypt because Herod wanted to destroy the child.
When Herod realized that the wise men weren't coming back, he reacted in a way that would cause indescribable agony in the lives of many others. We find in Matthew 2:16, *"Then Herod, when he saw that he was deceived by the wise*

*men, was exceeding angry; and he sent forth and put to death all the male children who were in Bethlehem and in all its districts, from two years old and under, according to the time which he had determined from the wise men."* Matthew Henry's commentary on this passage of scripture states that "whatever crafty, cruel devices are in men's hearts, the counsel of the Lord will stand." I'm sure Herod thought that his murderous decree had solved the problem, and yet his actions fulfilled one of the many prophecies surrounding Christ's birth, this one found in Jeremiah 31:15.

The point in this story that had previously gone somewhat unnoticed by me was that Herod's rage at the wise men was imposed against the most innocent of all, showing just how diabolical Satan's schemes are at any time. Herod worshiped himself and so there could be no room for the worship of God. It is also a challenge to consider how many times we misplace our frustration or anger. If we're having a bad day at home, do we take it out on our co-workers? If we've had to wait in line too long at a store, do we then endanger someone's life by driving crazily to get to our next destination? Do we take a moment to breathe and think through an answer before we text back too quickly, leaving a footprint that can't be reversed? Ask yourself this question – *"Was God was pleased with the way I responded to the last difficult situation I encountered?"*

Herod's reaction was brutal and horrific and yet we see how the persecution of Christ's kingdom began almost immediately after His birth. Satan isn't out just to cause us to have a bad day: he desires to "steal, kill, and destroy" anyone who has trusted in Christ for salvation. The manger was necessary for the cross. Pray for the persecuted Church all around the world, remember those suffering physically and emotionally, thank Him for the gift of His Son, and renew the perseverance it takes to live the Christian life in a society moving at light speed away from the truth of Him.

**What is God teaching me from today's devotional?**

# RECIPE FOR A DINNER OF HERBS

*"Better is a little with the fear of the Lord, than great treasure with trouble. Better is a dinner of herbs where love is, than a fatted calf with hatred."*
Proverbs 15:16-17

Cooking is one of the greatest forms of stress relief I know. For me, baking a cake or a pie or just trying out a new recipe is a source of inner enjoyment comparable to few other things. I think I enjoy cooking for many reasons, but most of all because I like to eat! It also makes me feel good to see my husband and son enjoying something delicious right out of the oven. My little boy will often say, *"That (food) is the best in the world."* Cooking also gives me the solitude of the kitchen, which is my own little world of being able to create new dishes or repeat the tried-and-true ones we love so much. I'm the only cook in our family so I have total rule over the food that comes out of it! I'm reminded, in the kitchen, of childhood memories of my Mama preparing wonderful, from-scratch, meals, and I'm so thankful that she took the time to teach me how to cook.

One of the many lessons I learned from my parents was how to make-do with what food we had on hand. As I was growing up, I watched my Daddy work very hard year after year to plant and tend a large vegetable garden. One year in particular, when money was tight, we practically lived solely on the food that came from our garden. Even so, my Mama and Daddy had a way of making our meals delicious and they also had a way of taking what seemed like a little and turning it into much more. In all truth, God always met our needs and provided for us even at times when it may have felt like there was very little. Even at these low points, my parents never once went without tithing and continued to give of themselves to others in need. I'm blessed beyond words by their example!

The writer of Proverbs tells us in today's passage how that even a little with the Lord is better than a large bank account with turmoil. I love Proverbs 15:17 where the description is of a *'dinner of herbs' with love* (or as one commentary described it, a dinner with a few vegetables) is esteemed higher than a sumptuous feast. No matter how little you feel you may be bringing to the proverbial table of your life, God promises that, with Him, a little with love is better than a lot with turmoil. Think of all the arguments, gossip, and unpleasant conversation that can be stopped by tempering your speech with a little love and kindness. Consider how a tender hug given to someone in a crisis tends to reassure them when they need it most. The smallest acts of compassion reap big rewards in God's economy because those are the things that truly matter.

God has a way of mysteriously multiplying the meager things we have into abundant blessings that cannot be explained. He promises to bless those who put Him first in their lives and can easily work miracles of provision, much like the woman in the Old Testament who was down to her last bit of oil. So then, a recipe for a dinner of herbs is made up of two parts: respect and reverence for God and love for others. Combine those two things with complete trust in His provision, and you'll find that you have a heavenly recipe for being completely satisfied with whatever is on your table. Then, give us Lord our daily bread. Amen.

**What is God teaching me from today's devotional?**

# CATFISH LASAGNA

*"Do not be unequally yoked together with unbelievers. For what fellowship has righteousness with lawlessness? And what communion has light with darkness?"*
II Corinthians 6:14

Certain things simply do not go together, as I was reminded in a humorous way the other day. Passing by a restaurant on my way to work, I noticed that the sign advertising their daily specials included an entrée I'd never had before. Due to the fact that the sign that was too small to properly give room for spacing, the restaurant was proudly promoting "CATFISH LASAGNA" as the delicacy of the day ☺ I laughed out loud as I thought of the innocent faux pas there for any passer-by to see. Perhaps the feline population may have been tempted, but the rest of us surely dare not think of what such a feast might look (or worse yet, taste) like...

Truly, some things just aren't meant to be paired together. In today's scripture, the Apostle Paul is giving a word of caution to Christians to avoid being caught up in unhealthy relationships with those who are unbelievers. Most commonly associated with marriage, this passage can rightly be applied to any relationship whereby we're joining in a close bond. I've read several commentaries on this section of Paul's second letter to the church in Corinth, and the common denominator appears clear to me: Christians aren't meant to be united in such a way with those outside the faith as to seem to be condoning or participating in a way of life that isn't honoring to God.

For instance, if you're a new Christian and your best friend is still an unbeliever, it will naturally become more and more difficult for a tight friendship to endure because you will want to draw closer to God, which will pull you away from anything that's opposed to the things of God. This is in no way meant to imply that we shouldn't be friends with or try to positively influence others outside the faith toward a relationship with Christ. Jesus was the best example of this as He regularly spent time around those who needed Him most. Jesus loved everyone and so should we, but we aren't to compromise our beliefs by engaging in anything that the Bible tells us is wrong. If someone asked you to go with them to worship an idol, you'd probably run. Yet if someone asked you to go see a movie that was going to put images and ideas into your mind that were completely dishonoring to God, would you run from that too? What if you used that opportunity to tell the person why you would choose otherwise?

While we naturally recoil at the thought of catfish lasagna, we don't always so naturally recoil at certain things that ought to cause us to do so. Take a moment to pray and ask God if there's anything in your life that's not lined up with what the Bible teaches. Let Him shine the light on any area that needs attention and then take the steps necessary to realign yourself with His will. As Christians, anything or anyone we're in close relationship with should be honoring to Him. If you find yourself in a situation completely beyond your control, pray and seek God's guidance and then continue to pray. Let the Holy Spirit guide you forward and then ask Him to replace anything that you've had to let go of with new, Christ-honoring relationships and habits. He will answer because He loves you.

**What is God teaching me from today's devotional?**

# SNOWY SEASONS

*"She is not afraid of snow for her household, for all her household is clothed with scarlet."*
Proverbs 31:21

Many of us have experienced beautiful winter days, complete with an abundance of snow and limited ability to leave home. These are the kinds of days that children dream about! We've all built snowmen, gone sledding, ate snow cream, made snow angels, had snowball fights, and enjoyed hot chocolate – all in the happy spirit of what snow days bring. We enjoy the snow while we can because it doesn't usually last very long, at least not in the South. Unfortunately, each year some face power outages, nearly impossible travel, and downed trees. For those times, snowy weather is more of a difficulty than an enjoyment. But even then, there's a solace that comes in these miniature periods of hiatus that isn't exactly replicated in other seasons of the year. Have you ever just sat and watched the snow falling in all its soft and feathery beauty and contemplated the uniqueness of each snowflake? What magnificence and power our God has to finely appoint each of His creations, even elements of weather, so precisely.

Did you know that the Bible specifically mentions snow about 25 different times? I've been particularly interested in today's verse from Proverbs where we see a godly woman's response to snow (or the rigors of a cold season). She isn't afraid because she knows that her family is, quite literally, protected by their strong and resistant clothing. One commentary I read said that the word used in the Hebrew implies that her family's clothing is "double layered" against the cold. They are prepared as much as they can be in the human sense, but speaking in a spiritual sense, they're also covered by God's grace. The Proverbs 31 woman has a family prepared against the cold seasons of life.

While we may enjoy the occasional snow day, many of us would grow weary if it lasted too long. In the same way, some seasons of life can feel like a cold day that has overstayed its welcome. In fact, many times we can almost begin to believe that our situation will never improve or that we must accept that our life is forever robbed of sunshine and warmth. This simply is not true. We can be protected from the difficulties of life by the covering of Christ over our lives. Christ tells us time and time again that He is our refuge as a safe place to weather the storms of life. I cannot imagine going through life without the protection of Christ.

Job 37:6 states, *"For He says to the snow, 'Fall on the earth'; likewise to the gentle rain and the heavy rain of His strength."* Here we see that God orders snow, as He does all weather. He is in control of winter just as He is all the other seasons. I sincerely hope that you're able to enjoy the snow and this respite time of year when it comes, but if you're facing a difficult season of life or even some days that feel bitterly bleak, I hope you'll turn your face to the warmth of God's loving protection and be renewed.

One of my all-time favorite quotes is attributed to C.S. Lewis. He wrote, *"God will not leave us in perpetual winter."* For many years, that quote sat at my desk and I would routinely think about the deep truth found in those words. God does indeed lead us through some snowy seasons, but the end result is always our good and His glory. He's guiding us to a deeper understanding of Him and a much, much brighter future ahead. Rest your head and your heart in the all-wise, all-providential, arms of Jesus. He will carry you through this and every season of your life.

**What is God teaching me from today's devotional?**

# MANNERS MATTER

*"Let your speech always be with grace, seasoned with salt, that you may know how you ought to answer each one."*
Colossians 4:6

*"A word fitly spoken is like apple of gold in settings of silver."*
Proverbs 25:11

One of the best bits of advice I received as a newly-married woman was to use good manners in my home. The older lady, who had been a Sunday School teacher and babysitter of mine as a child, passed along this wisdom adding that this would make my home a place of comfort and would carry my husband and I through many rough days. I recall thinking that the advice seemed a bit Victorian, but I truly did take it to heart. Unfortunately, I've had my share of less-than-gracious days, but overall I can say that my husband and I have always tried to show respect to one another by the use of good manners. Way beyond the practice of 'please' and 'thank you', the correct setting of a table, and writing timely thank you notes, all good manners are rooted in unselfish acts. Even the most impeccable hostesses (a la Downton Abbey) have their moments of weakness, but Christians have the truest example of all guiding our conduct - Jesus.

Nowadays, manners can seem purely subjective, meaning that manners are whatever a person chooses to make them. Many younger people have no idea who Emily Post was or what George Washington's <u>Rules of Civility and Decent Behavior</u> were meant to convey. Sadly, manners may even be twisted as a means to an end; if someone wants something badly enough, they many use good etiquette as a way to manipulate the situation in order to get the desired "something". While proper etiquette may be a learned and proper response, good manners come from the heart.

Today's verse from the Book of Colossians is a reminder that when we speak with wisdom and kindness, we will be best able to tell others of the love of Christ. The Wycliffe Bible Commentary states, "An offensive or insipid manner is not likely to accomplish much. Therefore, in life and speech the Christian witness should be appetizing..." Non-Christians should see that our words are laced with grace, wisdom, and love. Likewise, the scripture passage from Proverbs describes the use of a well-said, well-timed word as beautiful and pure. If we ever want others to see Christ shining through us, we need to be ready with gracious words. Having that sort of habit of speech, combined with considerate manners, may soften a heart that has otherwise been hardened.

Recently, I've been saying to my son on a daily basis, "Let's pray that every word we say be honoring to Christ and kind to others." That can feel like a tall order sometimes, and none of us are perfect; however, Christians are meant to communicate the truth of Christ's love in a way that would honor Him. This can only come about as we draw closer to the Lord, particularly in prayer and knowing His Word. He will place in our heart and minds the responses to difficult situations, and we never know what a day may bring. There may be days when this will seem relatively easy and other days when it takes everything within us to bite our tongues, not participate in gossip, or to refrain from a battle of words.

Here's a really meaningful challenge for the days ahead: Pray every morning, before you even get out of bed, that your words will be wise, gracious, and loving. Then step out into a day that brings no regret – a day in which your words are so uplifting and inspirational that others can't help but see Christ through them. Couple those words with unselfish, truly well-mannered behaviors, and you will be amazed at how effective you can be. When you lay your head down at night, thank the Lord for giving you the right words at the right time. May all our words and actions be as beautiful as golden apples in silver settings.

**What is God teaching me from today's devotional?**

# THOSE WEREN'T ENTIRELY COOKIES... AND OTHER DECEPTIONS

*"Woe to you, scribes and Pharisees, hypocrites! For you cleanse the outside of the cup and dish, but inside they are full of extortion and self-indulgence. Blind Pharisee, first cleanse the inside of the cup and dish, that the outside of them may be clean also. Woe to you, scribes and Pharisees, hypocrites! For you are like whitewashed tombs which indeed appear beautiful outwardly, but inside are full of dead men's bones and all uncleanness."*
Matthew 23:25-27

■■■■■■■■■■■■■■■■■■■■■■■■■■■■■■■■■■■■■■■

Last year, my son brought home a cute little iridescent bag of cookies he'd made that day in school. As part of a holiday party, the class had made no-bake cookies to give as gifts for their families. He insisted that I try one and, of course, I did. I took a bite and... time... stood... still... as my mind raced through the list of possible ingredients that my mouth had just tried to decipher. The only distinguishable taste was coconut – the rest was a total guess until it hit me... yes, I'm 99.9% sure that the one happy little no-bake cookie I'd eaten had been infused with a wee bit of playdough!

After reassuring myself that I wasn't going to die a horrible death by poisoning, I had a good laugh at the situation. Then quickly disposing of the remaining balls of goo, I made sure my son knew just how much I appreciated his hard work. That tasty little experience made me think of several things, but mostly of how often appearances can be deceiving.

One of my favorite BBC television shows is "Keeping Up Appearances", a huge hit from the early 90's in which a British housewife is determined to climb the social ladder despite her own family's working-class background. Hyacinth Bucket (pronounced Bouquet, to hear her tell it), is constantly finding herself in awkward (and hilarious) situations of her own making as she tries her hardest to appear a certain way. Though her home is spotless and her manners impeccable, she is constantly trying to disguise all the shortcomings in her life. While we laugh at the absurdity, we're also stung by the accuracy of how close to home the humor lands.

In today's scripture passage, Jesus explains that it may be possible to look beautiful on the outside and still be rotten on the inside. Now, there's nothing wrong with putting our best foot forward while relying on God to see us through some difficult times. In these cases, we are often smiling on the outside while our hearts are breaking under that exterior. That's not what this scripture is about. What we want to be on guard against is having unresolved sin in our lives, while pretending that we don't. This is also an admonition for us not to point to other people's shortcomings when we are secretly, or not so secretly, also living a life outside of God's will.

So whether in an innocent-looking little cookie or our own attempts at perfection, we may be deceived. Jesus *is* truth, and scripture reminds us over and over again that the truth will set us free. Won't you determine to live in truth? Be instead a woman unwilling to tell lies, unwilling to believe them, and fully reliant upon the truth of Christ.

**What is God teaching me from today's devotional?**

# GARAGE DOORS AND OUTLET MALLS

*"A man's heart plans his way, but the Lord directs his steps."*
Proverbs 16:9

*"...The Lord gave, and the Lord has taken away; blessed be the name of the Lord."*
Job 1:21b

■■■■■■■■■■■■■■■■■■■■■■■■■■■■■■■■■■■■■■■■■■

I'm a planner by nature, a trait which has served me fairly well throughout my life. I'm also married to a planner, which means that a lot of careful thought, preparation, and prayer has gone into big decisions, major purchases, and vacations over the years. As a couple, we budget and save, we pray through and plan, and we weigh options as wisely as we know how. All that said, and for all our good intentions, life is utterly unpredictable. Our best laid plans can be upended and disrupted at any time. Such was the case not too long ago...

One morning, after a last-minute, unexpected change in our routine schedule of getting out the door, I pulled out of the garage to take our son to school – only the garage door wasn't all the way open! In a matter of a few seconds, the sound of metal crunching, my son yelling from the back seat, and my husband staring in frustrated bewilderment all seemed to come together in one crescendo of agony for me. This was followed by my husband cutting his hand as he literally had to bend the metal garage door so that I could get the car out, and then when I did get my son to school I realized I'd forgotten his lunch. The whole day ended up unfolding into a series of unusual, unexpected, and unpleasant delays and expenses. Several times throughout that day, I thought of how peaceful the early morning had been; I had sat at my desk and had a wonderful early quiet time with the Lord. I hadn't known what a challenging day was just ahead of me, but Jesus certainly knew.

Just a few days after the garage door incident, I was able to spend a wonderful afternoon shopping at an outlet mall with my sister-in-law. We found some incredible, *and I truly mean incredible*, after-Christmas bargains and were actually able to put a dent in our *future* Christmas shopping (11 months in advance)! Later on that day, I thought about how unanticipated our bargain shopping savings had been and how wonderful it had been to have had my expectations interrupted, so-to-speak, for the good.

The Bible plainly tells us that, although we may plan and prepare, the Lord ultimately controls the outcomes. The Lord does give and the Lord does take away. Christ knows the very things we need and the things that we need to make us better and more like Him. We're also taught in the Bible to praise the Lord for the good and the bad. We are to fix our eyes on Him and lose the clenching grasp on our circumstances or else we run the risk of basing our happiness solely on how we feel or how things are working out for us. Ask most people how they're doing, and they base their answer on the latest thing or circumstance, not on the overall blessings in their life.

I pray that as this day or week unfolds, with all the expected and the unexpected, you will determine to praise the Lord through it all. If a tough situation rears its ugly head, meet it head-on, commit it to Christ, and resolve to thank God for what He's teaching you through it. Likewise, if a wonderful experience happens, remember to give the glory to God for the gifts He gives. This is sometimes easier said than done, but it's completely possible to develop a new way of thinking and reacting to surprises in your life. If you can picture God as having a perfect (and I mean perfect) blueprint for your day, your week, your life, and then picture Him fitting every single day into that plan, you will have a different outlook. Then join Him in that perfect plan by submitting to His authority in your life and thanking Him for the blessings and the setbacks because you acknowledge Him as wholly trustworthy. There is no telling what awaits as you yield to Him!

## What is God teaching me from today's devotional?

# PUTTING THE HOLIDAYS IN FOCUS

*"And the angel said unto them, Fear not: for, behold, I bring you good tidings of great joy, which shall be to all people."*
Luke 2:10

As my family put up our Christmas tree last year, I recall being very happy that chilly afternoon. It was a wonderful time, complete with all the trimmings: Gene Autry Christmas carols in the background, homemade hot cocoa, the smell of sugar cookies, and all of us happy and festive. I would even occasionally stop to play Christmas songs on the piano and my husband and son would sing along.

So what could possibly have sucked the joyous breath out of me on such a festive afternoon? It was a tiny little Christmas ornament purchased twelve years ago, which would have signified our first child's first Christmas. The little ornament in the shape of a cherub was wrapped loosely in a blanket of snowy white paper. I held that fragile little bit of porcelain closely in my hands and my heart ached all over again as I thought of our child, my only pregnancy, lost to miscarriage. All the painful memories of that time came flooding back in an instant. A few minutes later I noticed that my husband looked sad as he put up some of his parent's ornaments, and then I recalled that the past week had been the anniversary of his mother's death many years ago. We looked at each other in a knowing way and then hugged tightly for a few minutes without needing to say a word. For a split second, as I buried my head on his warm shoulder, I was gripped with the frightening thought that perhaps we wouldn't be able to enjoy Christmas at all. What if the sadness of things lost overshadowed all the good things we could celebrate?

What if our young son was deprived of some joy because we were so caught up in the past?

Later on that evening, I was still absorbed with the memory that small little ornament had evoked when I remembered the story of the birth of Jesus and the angelic admonition to the shepherds that solitary night over two thousand years ago. The shepherds were anxious and afraid at the sight of the angels, but they were told that Jesus' birth was bringing great joy to the world. Somehow that passage of scripture was like a soothing caress to my sad heart. Instead of thinking about what could have been, I was drawn to what the very angels from Heaven had said to those people who were frightened. Christ had come and nothing would ever be the same. He was bringing joy into a dark and burdened world.

Any holiday season can be difficult for many people. No matter how we've become separated from a loved one (divorce, empty nest, death, or a myriad of other reasons) that suffocating hurt is often made harder by the fact that we're 'supposed to be happy' at certain times of the year. If you find yourself among this number, I encourage you to read Luke chapter two with a fresh focus. Let God's Word remind you that Christmas is about Christ and that He wants to calm our anxious hearts. He came to reconcile us to God so that we might not live in fear or in despair. The shepherds immediately left to find the baby Jesus once the angels had disappeared from view. My prayer is that we will all seek Christ this and every holiday season, instead of dwelling too long on the past. When our holidays are filled with memories of Christ and what He has done for us, we can be truly content in the knowledge that He has come to bring joy and that His plan for us is a perfect one.

**What is God teaching me from today's devotional?**

# MY COUGH HURTS

*"The eternal God is your refuge, and underneath are the everlasting arms..."*
Deuteronomy 33:27a

When my son was about two years old, he awoke one night with a dry, hacking cough. He wasn't running a fever, but I could tell he didn't feel well. In fact, all he could relate to me was, *"My cough hurts, Mommy!"* I knew that he meant his throat was sore, but he wasn't able to explain the problem in grown-up terms. Though the cough was the symptom, he couldn't possibly understand that there was a deeper predicament. He just wanted the pain to go away.

How often do we find ourselves in a similar situation, unable to properly explain the hurt we feel? Sometimes we only see the symptom and don't stop to investigate the underlying problem. There are certain situations in which the best we can do is to just call His name or try to explain our breaking heart in one or two sentences of prayer. Thankfully, Christ understands our thoughts and knows what we need before we even ask Him. He also sees through eyes that penetrate straight into the root of all our anxieties and burdens and stands waiting with exactly the right cure.

Today's verse is one of the most beautiful word pictures in the Bible of how God upholds and takes care of His children. God is our refuge, and His arms will never fail to be there for us, underneath all the conscious and subconscious layers of our worries and insecurities. God has not only given us His promises, but He has equipped us, by faith, to endure circumstances and dilemmas that might almost seem impossible at times. I can recall a few times in my own life when I've had to literally picture Jesus holding my hand or walking beside me just to take the next step forward in the day. Thankfully, those very darkest days have always been followed by times of great peace and unexplainable comfort. I know that every single time I've been at my lowest point, Christ has intervened and helped me through.

Most women I know talk metaphorically from time to time about the need for a safety net. We plan for vacations, college tuition, retirement income, children, careers, and the list goes on and on. It's a Plan B mentality to help cope with Plan A. Unfortunately, many of us never plan for the day we're in or even the day ahead. We think of God waiting for us in the big, vast unknown, and yet we forget that He's there for us where we are now.

Stop where you are, in this minute of time, and consider your day. Do you realize that God is as close now as He will be, or has been, in those big, defining moments of your life? He never changes because He doesn't need to change: He is perfect and His everlasting arms never grow tired or distracted from the care of His children. You are safe. No matter how dark the night or how painful the day, light and comfort are found in Christ alone. Why not thank Him right now and go out in the peaceful knowledge that He will take care of you, as He always has and always will.

**What is God teaching me from today's devotional?**

# BLINDSIDED

*"Now the men who held Jesus mocked Him and beat Him. And having blindfolded Him, they struck Him on the face and asked Him, saying, 'Prophesy! Who is the one who struck You?' And many other things they blasphemously spoke against Him."*

Luke 22:63-65

Today's scripture describes a scene in which Jesus was being mocked by the soldiers and others who had taken Him prisoner, not long before He would be crucified on the cross. At one point, they blindfolded Jesus and began to hit Him. All the while, they were making fun of Him by asking Him to identify who had struck Him. Those inflicting the pain had actually made a game of thinking they were blindsiding Him with their blows. The truth was that Jesus had sacrificially submitted to God's Will in facing every awful moment leading up to His death and was far from blindsided. Ironically, though He allowed them to blindfold Him, He was the very one who had healed many blind people and given them sight.

As I read this story again, I was deeply moved as I thought about how Jesus knew everything about each person who hit Him that day. He knew everything about anyone who spit on Him or shouted an insult. He had given them the gift of life because He was their Creator, and yet He was silent as His tormentors beat, spit on, and ridiculed Him. At this point in the story of the cross, the pain and insults were only beginning. Jesus would go on to face horrific beatings, the agony of being betrayed, and the cruelty of the cross itself.

We often feel blindsided by hurts that seem to come out of nowhere. Most Christians can point to some instance in which they've been mocked or mistreated simply for being a Christ-follower. Whether it's for a moral stand we take on certain issues or because of activities we choose not to participate in, there seems to always be those who would like to cast us aside as irrelevant, old-fashioned, or fanatical. The Bible tells us in II Timothy 3:12, *"Yes, and all who desire to live godly in Christ Jesus will suffer persecution."* The word in the Greek text, *persecution*, actually means "to be hunted". While we aren't exempt *from* it, God does promise to deliver us *through* it. One of the greatest joys in life is to see God at work through our difficulties and then glorified in the end.

There is also the supreme comfort in knowing that, because Jesus died for our sins, we can accept Him as our Savior and be assured of a life with Him for eternity. We are still left with a tremendous responsibility for how we live the life He has given us – either fully surrendered to His will or just trying to remain lukewarm. We simply cannot compromise: we are either going to be effective Christians or ineffective. Don't you want to live a life that really counts for Christ? The peace that Christ gives is worth more than anything any fence-sitting life could afford.

The next time you face a situation (big or small) in which you can either stand for Christ or deny Him, please stand. No one else at the table may pray over their meal, but you can. Others may think it's ok to view something that in no way honors Christ, but you don't have to look at it. Some may say that picking up the Bible to read it once in a while is enough, but we need to be in His Word every day. Being a spiritual leader in your home is important so make sure your family is in a good, Bible-believing church each week. Show love to others and meet needs in confidential ways. These are only a few things that can really make a difference in how you show others what a true Christian really looks like. May we all be glowing reflections of our dear, sweet Savior!

**What is God teaching me from today's devotional?**

# BROKEN THINGS MADE NEW

*"But Mary stood outside by the tomb weeping, and as she wept she stooped down and looked into the tomb. And she saw two angels in white sitting, one at the head and the other at the feet, where the body of Jesus had lain. Then they said to her, 'Woman, why are you weeping?' She said to them, 'Because they have taken away my Lord, and I do not know where they have laid Him.'"*

John 20:11-13

My son's Sunday School teacher was supposed to have received a gift of three, hand-painted ceramic eggs this past Easter Sunday; however, she only received two… That is because, just as we were leaving for church that morning, the basket the eggs were in fell out in the car and one of them broke. As my husband reached down to pick it up, a sharp edge cut him and he had to go back inside to bandage his finger. I should also have mentioned that moments before all this happened, I had locked us out of the house in a rush to take a few pictures to commemorate the day. A little later, I laughed as the photos that we'd taken in no way showed the struggles of the morning. There we stood in our Easter best, smiling as if it was a perfect day!

The broken egg and the other mishaps of that morning made me think about how often we miss the bigger picture by focusing on ourselves. If we had allowed it, the obstacles and setbacks of that morning could have resulted in an argument with my husband and child, additional frustration, and maybe even deciding to stay at home instead of going on to church. Thankfully, we were able to see the string of unfortunate events as just that and no more, and were able to get past it pretty quickly.

I love the passage of scripture in John 20:11-18 in which the Bible tells us that Mary Magdalene was so concerned with her own grief and her search for Jesus' body that she nearly forgot Jesus' promise that He would indeed rise again. In the garden, Mary spoke to the two angels but didn't even wait for them to say that Jesus had risen. She wandered around through the garden and did eventually see Jesus, not as the gardener she had first supposed, but as the risen Lord. Mary had been a broken person at one time, but had been made whole by her faith in Christ. She became a new woman because she believed and followed Jesus. It would have been very hard for her to have seen Him put to death, and I'm sure that the days between the cross and the empty tomb were full of wondering and fear. How kind and loving of the Lord to appear to her and to give her the task of telling the disciples that Jesus had risen!

I pray that every Easter season for you is one of somber remembrance of the cross and a joyful celebration of the resurrection. I also hope it is a time of reflection on your life and your relationship with Christ. I'm so thankful that Easter is more than chocolate, eggs, new clothes, and lunch with family and friends. The absolute essence of our Christian faith is that we serve a risen Christ and that we have the promise of eternal life, more beautiful and real beyond anything our minds could possibly conceive.

So, if something in your life is broken or feels tangled in a knot of anxiety, remember that Christ cares and is your risen Savior, not just now but for eternity. He is the expert at untangling the dilemmas of this life. You can trust Him, depend upon Him, rely on Him, and talk with Him. He gave us His Word and we can speak to Him in prayer. What joy we could have if we truly lived in this confidence every moment of every day!

**What is God teaching me from today's devotional?**

# WHERE ARE YOU GETTING YOUR ADVICE?

*"...a word spoken in due season, how good is it!"*
Proverbs 15:23b

We all need some type of counsel from time to time, whether it be for a personal or business matter, a work-related issue, or just good, old-fashioned, common-sense advice. When I'm asked for advice of a personal nature, I try to always apply Biblical principles to the suggestions I give, and that has served me well. The Bible has a lot to say about wise counsel and the difference between good and bad advice. All of us have, at some time in our life, been on both sides of the guiding and advising issue; sometimes we're dispensing advice and other times we're the recipients of it. *Be so careful of both the guidance you give and the guidance you take!*

The guiding principal of wise counsel is wisdom, and we're told in Proverbs 9:10, *"The fear of the Lord is the beginning of wisdom: and the knowledge of the Holy is understanding."* Simply put, there is a higher perspective that comes from God, and the only way we can share in this is to know Him intimately through His Word and prayer.

The book of Proverbs is full of the principals of wise counsel. Proverbs 15:23b says, *"...a word spoken in due season, how good is it!"* Think before you speak, and if you don't know what to say don't say anything. At those times when you're the one in need of direction, make sure you're praying about it and seeking Godly counsel. I'm amazed at how many Life Coaches and Career Counselors are employed these days. There is definitely a need for this type of guidance in some cases, but many people only ever go to others and never to God. Our dilemmas are important to us, yet we often feel that we can't make decisions without asking all of our friends for their opinions before we ever come before God with our needs. *Remember, truly wise counsel will never conflict with anything in God's Word.*

A quick word about questionable advice: just because a person has been through a similar situation to you doesn't mean they're always going to give wise counsel. Sometimes the best advice is the cautionary tale of what to avoid. Also, proceed very cautiously when giving direction. There's an old quote by Hannah Whitall Smith, *"The true secret of giving advice is, after you have honestly given it, to be perfectly indifferent whether it is taken or not and never persist in trying to set people right."* God is the discerner of all our thoughts and intents. Leave it in His hands.

Lastly, Isaiah 9:6 identifies the greatest counselor, *"For unto us a child is born, unto us a son is given: and the government shall be upon his shoulder: and his name shall be called Wonderful, Counselor, The mighty God, The everlasting Father, The Prince of Peace."* Even as a prophetic mention, Jesus is given the title of Counselor. He calmed the seas, healed the blind, took our sins upon Himself on the cross, and rose to make intercession for us. Why then would we not go to Him first? The next time you're in need of guidance or you're attempting to give it, consider the awesome importance of Godly counsel. Make sure you don't answer or respond too quickly; pray and ask for godly wisdom before moving forward. Then, with the Bible and prayer as your guides, move forward in faith, confident that our Good Shepherd will never lead us astray.

**What is God teaching me from today's devotional?**

# COULD BE WORSE

*"Do all things without complaining and disputing, that you may become blameless and harmless, children of God without fault in the midst of a crooked and perverse generation, among whom you shine as lights in the world..."*
Philippians 2:14-15a

As a child, one of my very favorite books was <u>Could Be Worse</u> by James Stevenson. As an adult, I've read it countless times to my son, and its cover is even the screensaver on my home computer. It's a humorous, lesson-teaching book about an unexcitable grandfather who never has anything interesting happen to him and always tells his grandchildren, *"Could be worse!"* in response to whatever calamity they encounter. Finally, one morning, he tells his grandchildren about the most amazing adventure he has just had the night before. The majority of the book is the grandfather recounting his series of unfortunate adventures, to which the children respond at the end by saying, *"Could be worse!"* The illustrations and story are top notch, in my opinion, and the lesson is clear that most every difficult thing that happens to us falls into the *'Could be worse'* category.

I've been guilty many times of using over-the-top words to describe a situation. I find myself describing something as *awful* or *the worst thing ever* when actually it may have only been a flat tire or a sinus infection. It seems funny as I write this, but it's true that we often exaggerate the negative significance of a situation because, at that moment, it is the thing we're most focused on resolving. In no way am I taking away from the deepest heartaches of life, but, truth be told, while there are absolutely very hard times that we all have to endure, most of our day-to-day dilemmas are more nuisances as opposed to major problems. We lose perspective in the moment.

The Bible is clear that we should not be complainers, and in today's passage, the reason for that is so that we will shine as lights reflecting the light of Christ. If we refuse to complain and argue unnecessarily, we are showing others that we have faith in the design of our lives because it comes from the God of all creation. The more we trust the Lord with the setbacks, disappointments, and stressful situations we encounter, the more apt we will be to submit in each trial as though it were meant for our good and His glory. After all, every single trial we face carries with it the promise that if we will give it to Him and remain obedient and prayerful, good will come. As Romans 8:28 says, *"And we know that all things work together for good to those who love God, to those who are the called according to His purpose."* All things, means just that: <u>all</u> <u>things</u>. Some things do take longer than others, but the promise is the same.

The next time you're inclined to think that your situation is the worst thing ever or that you will never make it through the season of life you're facing, remember that complaining is not the answer. Prayer and dependence upon God to see you through is the only way you'll be able to successfully weather the storms of life. There is absolutely nothing that can take the place of surrender to Christ – not your career, not your healthy lifestyle, not your income, not your family, and not your circle of friends. Only Christ can give you the soul-level peace and security that is not dependent upon circumstances. Let's thank God today for all the things in our life that we've been spared and then *'Could be worse'* will take on a whole different meaning.

**What is God teaching me from today's devotional?**

# FEAR AND CHRISTMAS

*"And the angel said unto them, Fear not; for, behold, I bring you good tidings of great joy, which shall be to all people."*
Luke 2:10

Christmas is supposed to be a scene straight out of a Normal Rockwell painting, right? As I watch tragedy after tragedy in 30 second snippets on the news, I'm torn between anguish and apathy. Part of me wants to retreat inside the four walls of my home and believe that everything is safe and secure everywhere, and yet I'm more inclined to feel the agony of knowing that this world is engulfed in distress. We all have needs, and those needs are accompanied by the fear that they won't be met.

Lest we ever think we're all alone in this world that seems to be spinning out of control, allow me to remind you of the central characters of the Christmas story who all faced their own uncertain futures:

**Elizabeth & Zacharias** – were afraid they'd never have a child, but God gave them John the Baptist when all hope seemed lost.
**Mary** – was afraid when the angel came to her. The calling seemed impossible.
**Joseph** – was afraid of public opinion in marrying a woman ready to have a child that wasn't his.
**The Shepherds** – were literally terrified when they were surrounded by angels on that dark Judean hillside announcing Jesus' birth.
**King Herod** – was afraid the rumors he'd heard of a boy king would usurp his authority.
**The Wise Men** – were afraid of Herod's treachery and avoided returning to see him with the news of The Child.

Great scholars and thinkers, hymn writers and orators throughout the centuries have acknowledged the aspect of fear at this holy time of year. Take, for instance, one of the lines from O Little Town of Bethlehem – *"the hopes and fears of all the years are met in thee tonight."* There was hope, but there was fear. Of course! Of course there was fear being sowed at every turn because Satan was determined to destroy Christ. One of his most ancient tools of defeat is fear in the hearts of Believers. We are reminded again and again in the Bible to "Fear Not". The cure for fear is trust. Hebrews 2:15, *"and might free those who through fear of death were subject to slavery all their lives."* There is a correlation between slavery and fear just as there is between trust and freedom.

While I can't give all the answers to senseless tragedies and I can't control the future, I do absolutely **know**, beyond a shadow of a doubt, that Christ is in control. As Corrie Ten Boom, Nazi death camp survivor, said so beautifully, "There is no panic in Heaven, only plans." When you're tempted to turn your eyes to a dark shadow of fear lurking in a corner, raise your head to the sun and proclaim, like Mary in Luke 2:49, *"for the Mighty One has done great things for me; And holy is His name."* Fear Not!

**What is God teaching me from today's devotional?**

# STARTING OVER...AGAIN

*"Strength and honor are her clothing; She shall rejoice in time to come."*
Proverbs 31:25

It was the day after Christmas when I found myself with an unexpected, but not completely unfamiliar, tinge of sadness. The holiday season had rushed past me in a blur of lights, beribboned presents, and ageless carols. All that was left was the feeling that a new year was just around the corner and I was being forced to join its ranks marching forward in time. All that day and into the next I found myself thinking that I didn't want to say goodbye to the Christmas season because I wasn't sure what the new year would bring.

The past year has brought happiness, sadness, difficulty, dilemma, anxiety, growth, and hope. When I looked back at the previous year, I experienced some of a lot of things and a lot of others. I attended weddings and funerals, graduations and memorials, birthday parties and holiday gatherings, and many other mile markers of life. I watched friends and loved ones agonize over heartaches that seem to never mend, and I've felt helpless just sitting on the sidelines wishing I had the power to make it all right. I did actually keep my one and only New Year's resolution from last January 1st, which is nothing shy of a minor miracle. I also got a few do-over's and was able to start over, in a sense, with respect to a few things. In short, the triumphs and disappointments of the past year in my life wouldn't make a headline anywhere, but they were still mine.

A new year also begs the question of whether or not we'll formally resolve to do things differently or better. Resolutions are best called good intentions and I hope that if you make one you're likewise able to keep it. I'm personally in favor of resolutions that stretch us a bit. While the most popular will probably always be to lose weight, save money, and reduce stress, there are also some really fun ideas too. For instance: I resolve to <u>visit every historical landmark within a 25-mile radius of my home</u>, <u>eat at a new restaurant once each month</u>, <u>research my family ancestry</u>, <u>create a space in my home that is organized with all my important information</u>, <u>create a day dedicated to each family member once a month and let them pick their favorite things that day</u>, <u>take a lesson or two to decide if you'd like to learn more about art, music, a hobby, etc.</u> In other words, don't put off pursuing something you may end up really loving!

    Looking forward may be a source of anxiety or of hope. When we hold open our palms to the Lord and show Him all the things we try so desperately to clutch, He takes our need for control and hands us back His peace. So as I read those beautiful words again, Proverbs 31:25 seems to be written just for me, "Strength and honor are her clothing; She shall rejoice in time to come." Yes, there is a time to come in which we will all rejoice! No matter how dark your day may seem, remember that there is always hope for the Christian. The strength and the honor come from Christ in the same way the rejoicing belongs to Him also. One quote that helped me through some very dark days a few years ago is credited to C.S. Lewis. Lewis wrote, "God will not leave us in perpetual winter." Whatever 'winter' you're facing, remember that you WILL rejoice in time to come.

**What is God teaching me from today's devotional?**

# CONNECTIONS WITH GREATNESS

*"Let nothing be done through selfish ambition or conceit, but in lowliness of mind let each esteem others better than himself. Let each of you look out not only for his own interests but also for the interests of others."*
Philippians 2:3

In Charles Dickens' famous novel, *Our Mutual Friend*, he includes as minor characters a couple by the name of Mr. and Mrs. Veneering. These two, appropriately named for their veneer of nouveau wealth and influence, are described as people living way beyond their means and obsessed with trying to impress their so-called friends and acquaintances. Everything they're depicted as doing is an effort to advance themselves up the social ladder so that others will look at them and be impressed. Dickens masterfully pokes holes in the Veneering's pretentious behavior in an attempt to show the shallowness of their pretend life. The Veneering's finally end up in bankruptcy and are forced to move away.

Have you ever been around a name-dropper? Have you ever been one? Ouch! These are people who are eager to tell you all about who they know, as if their relationship is more than it is in actuality. The names they mention are their idea of influential, powerful, or wealthy people. If it's a name-dropper in the workplace, they mention those in top leadership positions; if in the community, it's only those who are well-connected or in some other type of prominent position. The Dictionary of American Slang's definition for a name-dropper is: *"one who ostentatiously mentions the names of important people as if they were friends and associates."* The irony is that most people who name-drop are really not close with any of the people they mention. At best, they're only peripheral associates, and the use of name-dropping is self-serving. The unconscious strategy underlying this behavior almost always betrays name-droppers for what they are really seeking, which is personal validation.

We all have varying degrees of connections with great people, whether it be a relative, a friend, or just an acquaintance; many of us know people who have made it big, so to speak, or have some extraordinary measure of success in life. It is a wonderful thing to have these types of personal or social connections, but it's an entirely different thing to use those relationships as a way to self-promote on the backs of others. Isn't it encouraging to hear people compliment others for the character traits that really matter: honesty, integrity, self-sacrifice, kindness, etc. In my opinion, the opposite of name-dropping is name-exalting (shout-out's), not to bring attention to ourselves but rather to bring attention to others. What a world it would be if, as today's scripture reminds us, we were preoccupied with finding ways to make other's lives better that we quit worrying about our own problems! Humility is the key because only a truly humble person can set their own interests aside in order to help someone else.

Hopefully we have some exceptional examples of strong Christians in our life – people who are committed to fulfilling God's purposes, at the expense of material success or career notoriety. I hope we seek out these types of relationships as vital to our growth in spiritual maturity. And don't forget that the ultimate connection with greatness comes from our relationship with Christ. He, and none other, can meet the needs we all have for real significance in this life. After all, putting others first is the example Jesus modeled for us as He taught that the first would be last and the last, first.

**What is God teaching me from today's devotional?**

# UNNAMED VALLEYS OF DESPAIR

*"Search me, O God, and know my heart; try me, and know my anxieties..."*

Psalm 139:23

There may be nothing harder than dealing with fear, worry, and anxiety because its grip on the mind can feel positively debilitating. Whether it's an all-out panic attack or just a recurring fearful or worrisome thought that has deep roots, we all struggle with some form or another of anxiety during our lifetime. Though it's much more common than gets talked about in open conversation, there is still an unfortunate stigma around expressing our battles with anxiety. It's sometimes viewed as a weakness - a crack in our psychological armor that alienates us from everyone else who we mistakenly believe clearly has it all together. It's hard to imagine that anyone could possibly be dealing with the same things we are because everyone else *looks* calm and secure. We unwittingly adopt a social media view of normal by seeing the dressed up version of others' lives.

We keep a lot of things quiet, don't we? We don't want to be perceived as having 'a real problem' or being 'unable to cope', and still so many people suffer in silence without support of family or friends, simply because the fear of admitting that something is beyond our control would be socially unacceptable. It feels ok to talk about other people's problems and other people's struggles, but our own issues are off-limits entirely. Simply put, we can't handle the truth of our own situations nearly as well as we'd like to think we do.

During times of fear, worry, and anxiety, we can be easily tempted to question why God would allow those awful feelings and then, before we know it, we're questioning our faith. After all, if our faith were stronger, would we even battle these issues at all? The truth is that none of us live in perfect bodies; we struggle with all sorts of different things. Walk the aisles of any drug store and think about the over-the-counter options for nearly every kind of ailment imaginable. This doesn't touch all the medications available by prescription. None of us are battling exactly the same problem in the same way. I think fear and anxiety is much the same. Even though there are clearly some common denominators, everyone is still managing through their own situation the best they know how. This is a great opportunity for me to say that a good Christian counselor is worth his/her weight in gold and there is no shame in seeking out their help. Even if you can't name what you're feeling, there is help available!

As I write this, I'm at a loss for answers to all these questions, but I do know there are certain absolute truths we can count on during times of struggle. First of all, God never changes; He is perfect, therefore He has no need to change. Next, He asks us to bring Him our worries, anxieties, and fears in order that He might handle them as He sees fit (I Peter 5:7). He wants us to pray fervently about the things we need. He doesn't promise a problem-free life, but He does promise to walk with us through our dark valleys AND He tells us not to worry about the future. Lastly, God is always at work behind the scenes of our life in order to bring about our good and His glory. Something you've struggled with may be exactly what someone else needs to hear to pull them off the island of isolation and back onto shore with others who openly admit that they don't have it all together but they're trusting their Savior.

These are hard days for many, and we need each other desperately. Please be honest, kind, and loving toward everyone; you never know the hard battle they may be facing, and you may be a true difference-maker in their life. If someone should speak to you in a way that has put them in a vulnerable position, be all the more Christ-like in your responses and pray with them, share encouraging scriptures, and keep checking in with them if possible. As Isaiah 61:3b states so beautifully, *"...to give them beauty for ashes, the oil of joy for mourning."* Only Christ can take the awfulness of anything and turn it into something beautiful. I pray you find comfort today.

**What is God teaching me from today's devotional?**

# TO REGIFT OR NOT REGIFT, THAT IS THE QUESTION

*"As each one has received a gift, minister it to one another, as good stewards of the manifold grace of God."*
I Peter 4:10

The other day I enjoyed a lighthearted conversation with a friend regarding the topic of regifting. Over coffee, we talked about whether or not we'd ever regifted something we'd been given and whether or not it was really so wrong to do so. Taboo or just marginally unacceptable, regifting is generally given a mild social no-no, although I'm pretty sure most of us have done it somewhere along the way. I certainly have!

We regift for many reasons: we already have one, we don't need it, we don't like it, or we find ourselves in a pinch and need to quickly find something to give someone else. The worst nightmare of regifting is that we might actually give someone *back* the same thing they gave us. EEK! That would be bad...

I was thinking about the regifting conversation I'd had with my friend as I was putting away the last of my Christmas decorations last year. It occurred to me that many aspects of the Christmas holidays are like gifts given over and over again. We box up our ornaments, decorations, and nativity sets only to bring them out next season as if they're brand new all over again. The thing that struck me most deeply was that regifting is really an act of keeping the gift going. It also made me pause to think about how we use the gifts that have been given to us.

The ultimate gift, Jesus, is like no other. He came to give us life and life more abundantly. Through His death on the cross for our sins, He provided the way of salvation so that we could enter into an eternal relationship with God. He also gave us certain gifts that we're to use for His glory. How are you using your gifts? Every gift (sometimes referred to as talents, special abilities, knacks, and natural skills) is a gift from God. The Bible clearly tells us in James 1:17a, *"Every good gift and every perfect gift is from above..."* Put another way, we are given our gifts and talents specifically to regift them!

Can you imagine someone musically gifted never singing or playing an instrument? What about someone gifted with teaching others who never once tried to help instruct? Can you imagine Rembrandt choosing to keep his art to himself or Charles Dickens never having *A Christmas Carol* published or Julia Child never cooking a soufflé for anyone? It seems absurd. While we aren't all gifted in the same way, we are specifically gifted with just what God wanted us to have to glorify Him. You could say we have a responsibility to regift; we are meant to pay it forward.

I challenge you this week to think about the gifts you've been given and then honestly ask the Lord how you might use your talents and abilities to honor Him even more this year. Then you can set about to ask the Lord for opportunities and avenues to share your gifts with others, all to the glory of God. What a wonderful way to regift!

**What is God teaching me from today's devotional?**

# A THOUGHT AFAR OFF

*"O Lord, You have searched me and known me. You know my sitting down and my rising up; You understand my thought afar off."*
Psalm 139: 1-2

I've always been something of a daydreamer. As a student in school, I can remember teachers all through the years reprimanding me for staring out a window, lost in thought. I've also frequently been a nighttime dreamer. In fact, most mornings I awake remembering some dream I had the night before; dreaming is a very normal thing for me. But one thing I've found is that dreams can be very difficult, sometimes nearly impossible, to explain to others. A time or two I've been trying to describe a dream I've had to my husband and have given up as I realized that my words really weren't properly explaining what I had seen in my sleep.

Many years ago, I fell in love with Psalm 139:2, in which we're told that God understands our far-off thoughts. Psalm 139 is one of the most beautiful chapters in all of the Bible as it intimately details the love and care God has for His children. In this chapter, we see time and time again that God has a perfect understanding of us. This particular psalm of David was written during a time of opposition (vs. 19-22), and yet it shows how thoroughly God knows us and is with us. In the first two verses we see how not only does God know what we're doing, but He also understands our thoughts, even the far-off ones.

We all have far-off thoughts. We have hopes and dreams that may be only known to us. Perhaps you've been unable to share some of your ideas with anyone else, and yet there's such a comfort in knowing that God not only knows, but understands those thoughts. Because He created us (vs. 13-16), He divinely chose all aspects of our being – our looks, our abilities, and our gifts. He created us as unique people, designed to bring Him glory.

He also understands our dreams and all the things that we really would love to accomplish or see come to fruition. If those dreams are in line with His perfect will for us, His plan will be accomplished through our obedience to Him.

Hopefully your home and work environment is a place where your thoughts and opinions can be openly shared and appreciated. However, if you live or work in a situation that doesn't place as much significance on this type of open communication, take solace in knowing that God understands and values your thoughts. Not only does He love to talk with you through prayer, but He truly *understands* your thoughts. It is an amazing privilege that God is interested in our deepest thoughts and most private needs. Sometimes we all have situations and feelings that are hard to explain to others, or they're not the sort of thing we feel comfortable in sharing. Remember that you can always tell Jesus. Psalm 139:17, *"How precious also are your thoughts to me, O God! How great is the sum of them!"* Just think, He has you on His mind even now. Take a moment today to thank Him for his love for you, and take great comfort in knowing that you are understood.

Henry Ward Beecher beautifully wrote, *"Thou understandest my thought. Before men we stand as opaque beehives. They can see the thoughts go in and out of us, but what work they do inside of a man they cannot tell. Before God we are as glass beehives, and all that our thoughts are doing within us He perfectly sees and understands."* Truly, no one can see the inner workings of our minds, but God not only sees, He *perfectly* understands. So, the next time you daydream about something that would be hard for you to explain to anyone, remember that your Creator knows all about you, loves you, and asks that you trust Him with every single part of your life.

**What is God teaching me from today's devotional?**

# EVERYTHING IN ITS PLACE

*"For God is not the author of confusion but of peace..."*
I Corinthians 14:33a

From time to time, I go through seasons of wishing I was one of those women whose closets, kitchen pantries, and linen cabinets were color coordinated, labeled, and regularly maintained. The items in my closet aren't arranged in order of season or color, although I do try to keep dresses in one section and everything else in another. My t-shirt drawer has, by some miraculous means, managed to stay a t-shirt drawer, although I recently retrieved some hidden Easter eggs out of there! I have towels that were wedding gifts fifteen years ago (which is why I still have them), and many other things that I have every intention of doing something with but just never seem to get around to it. Even with my fair share of cleaning things out and getting rid of clutter, I still seem to always have "collections" of mismatched things in piles at the end of my kitchen counter and dresser. The struggle is real ☺

A few years ago, I bought a book on organization and even managed to suffer through the accompanying video before deciding that it all seemed somewhat beyond my ability to make happen. Needless to say, I never invested in a label-maker or a matching set of storage boxes. While I'm secretly envious of my friends who have special containers for their spaghetti and clearly pigeon-holed spice cabinets, there is a method to how I have things stored away. I pretty much know where everything is, and that's all that matters most days. As I like to say, *"Everything is clean, at least!"*

In today's scripture verse, we see that we serve a God of order, not confusion. He has a plan and a purpose that is completely without turmoil. In fact, He is the Author of peace. There is no disorder where God is concerned because all that He does fosters harmony and unity. We mess things up when we try to get ahead of God or to act without Him as our guide, thus causing all sorts of chaotic situations. Like the piles of mismatched things that we don't know how to sort out or untangle, our lives can quickly become confused and misdirected when not placed at the feet of Jesus for Him to arrange. We try so hard, but all the trying in the world won't amount to peaceful results until we've surrendered our plans, goals, and dreams to the perfect will of God. Jesus tells us time and time again to bring Him our troubles and questions so that He can exchange those for His peace and comfort. What a great trade! He knows we can't possibly handle this life without Him because we weren't created to do so.

    I heard someone ask the question recently, *"What would you change if the doors to all your cabinets and closets were removed and everything was visible all the time?"* Most of us shudder at the very thought, but think for a moment about what you'd change if everyone could see your heart. Would they find confusion or peace, pretense or genuine honesty? We could all use the rearranging and reorganizing that Christ brings when we earnestly seek His plan for our lives. There will always be some evidence in a Christian's life of the power and light that Jesus gives but many of us are so busy and disorganized in the way we live that our light to others is dim. Every one of us could use some organizing and reprioritizing when it comes to our spiritual life. Because we're flawed and imperfect, we're all on a journey to be more like Christ in this life, but it takes discipline and dependence upon Him. I pray that all of us will commit today to however Christ wants to use us for His good and our glory so that our light will shine brightly wherever we go.

**What is God teaching me from today's devotional?**

# BEAUTY ALL AROUND US

*"One thing I have desired of the Lord, that will I seek; that I may dwell in the house of the Lord all the days of my life, to behold the beauty of the Lord, and to inquire in His temple."*
Psalm 27:4

▪▪▪▪▪▪▪▪▪▪▪▪▪▪▪▪▪▪▪▪▪▪▪▪▪▪▪▪▪▪▪▪▪▪▪▪▪▪▪▪▪▪▪▪▪

Beauty is such a subjective word these days. Most of the time it's used to describe a 5'10" model who wears a size 4, has flawless skin, perfect health, and all the right features of hair, face, and body to make everyone else pale in comparison. I did a quick experiment of sorts the other day in line at the grocery store as I glanced at the covers of several well-known magazines. I counted the word "beauty" on the covers of over 12 magazines, for a total of 23 times. In every instance, beauty was in reference to our personal appearance or the appearance of our home or other belongings. Not once was there a reference to the beauty within.

The beauty of the Lord is expressed in many ways throughout the Bible: His character, His mercy, and His lovingkindness are all beautiful to those who love Him. As David so poetically described in Psalm chapter 27, the beauty of the Lord was something he strongly desired to see. This type of beauty is akin to delight or pure joy. Many people describe the cross of Christ as beautiful, and that is because beauty here is associated with victory. There was joy at the cross, despite all the brutality and agony, because of the sacrifice made and the resulting freedom for all who will believe in Christ.

Have you ever been at a loss for words at something purely beautiful? Several years ago, my husband and I visited the area of Banff, in the majestic Canadian Rockies. The beauty of that place felt somewhat beyond description, and even photos or video failed to convey what my heart felt while looking out over the Bow River Valley as the first snow of October was falling. I remember saying aloud, 'How could anyone see this beauty and not believe in God?" There are other examples of indescribable beauty like seeing your child for the very first time or being reunited with someone after a long separation. There is also beauty in smiling through tears or enduring something you never thought you could. Consider the beauty in the petals of a rose, the rushing of a stream, or the invisible whisper of the wind.

For a Christian, the heart experience of Christ is a thing of unmatched beauty. The Bible reminds us that God has placed a desire within everyone for eternity, and that can't be satisfied with anything temporal. Ecclesiastes 3:11, *"He has made every thing beautiful in its time; also He has put eternity in their hearts, except that no one can find out the work that God does from beginning to end."* God makes things beautiful in His time. A situation that today may look hopeless may one day be a beautiful memory after being rightly placed within the framework of God's divine plan for your life.

From a practical point of view, look around you today and take a quick survey of what is beautiful. I think it's both encouraging and important to have things around you that bring joy and delight. Here are just a few suggestions to bring a little beauty to your home or workspace: framed photos of those you love, fresh flowers, a child's artwork, a daily calendar with inspirational quotes or Scripture verses, a sentimental charm or other piece of jewelry, great smelling soaps or perfumes, etc. These gentle reminders will hopefully prompt us to remember where true beauty originates.

There is beauty all around us, and it helps us to recognize it. Remember, too, that true beauty lies within a heart totally committed to Christ. That kind of beauty shines through in a way that can't be contained. True beauty isn't found in a wardrobe or in your makeup drawer, even though those things can be nice, but rather in the reflection of Christ in us. Take time today to search for beauty, genuine beauty, in obscure places as well as in the ordinary. You will find it.

**What is God teaching me from today's devotional?**

# THE REARVIEW MIRROR

*"...but one thing I do, forgetting those things which are behind and reaching forward to those things which are ahead, I press toward the goal for the prize of the upward call of God in Christ Jesus."*
Philippians 3:13b-14

■■■■■■■■■■■■■■■■■■■■■■■■■■■■■■■■■■■■■■

When I was 34 years old I had to have a radical hysterectomy due to severe endometriosis. It was the bitter end to many years of awful pain, fatigue, and unanswered questions. For my husband and I, there was a tragic element to the surgery since we'd tried for several years to have a child and had been to numerous doctors and spent thousands of dollars in attempts to conceive. We had experienced the joy of one pregnancy and then the subsequent anguish of miscarriage. The whole experience of the hysterectomy felt like a failure, a dream destroyed, and the end of possibility. I will never forget signing the required document at the doctor's office acknowledging that I understood that my hysterectomy would forever prevent me from conceiving a child. I wrote in my journal around that time that I was "walking around in a daze of unanswered prayers", as the light at the end of the tunnel grew dim.

In the days following the surgery, lying in the hospital bed, I fought the agony and despair as much as I fought the pain, but one thing my husband said to me during that time helped me tremendously. Every day, many times a day, he would say, *"Scarlett, this surgery is one day further in the rearview mirror. We're moving forward now."* At that time, we had already been waiting two years with an adoption agency, but all along I had just been sure that God would allow me to conceive. After all, I was praying so hard, seeking Him at every turn, and trying my best to praise Him despite all the setbacks. When it didn't turn out the way I had expected, I was confused, heartbroken, and flat-out exhausted.

As the days turned into months, which turned into years, I gradually learned that God's plan wasn't dependent upon my timetable; His perfect will was being worked in secret and His design was one that crossed many hurdles and stretched my faith in ways I was sure would nearly break me. Yet, always, ALWAYS, at my lowest points, He was there. I could write an entire book of all the ways God showed Himself to me during those times. I learned to refer to each letdown and heartbreak along that journey as simply, "in the rearview mirror", and then moved forward. Even when it felt a struggle to put one foot in front of the other, God provided the strength for me to do so.

Whatever you're facing today, and whatever you're struggling to leave behind, I pray that you'll think on today's scripture verses and try to leave the past behind as you stretch forward, in faith, toward your future. I know how hard it can be to endure, but the path to healing and maturity only come about when trials are rightly seen as God's perfect handiwork in your life. He wants you to trust Him, simply trust Him.

God did indeed bless us later with the indescribably beautiful gift of our son, and His perfect working in that situation was like the windows of Heaven had opened and angels of mercy had surrounded us. God knew, from before time, what the plan was for my life. He knows the plan for your life too. Won't you trust Him and leave the past in the rearview mirror? Brighter, sunnier days are ahead!

**What is God teaching me from today's devotional?**

CPSIA information can be obtained
at www.ICGtesting.com
Printed in the USA
LVOW12s0840220816

500918LV00005BA/8/P